CHAOS TO CURED

A Tale of Defeating Bipolar

By
Kirk Miller

PREFACE

Over ten years ago I overcame and defeated the bipolar that had been ripping my life apart. Reaching full remission is a statement I don't make lightly. As the first medically documented case, utilizing a unique medication protocol, I stand before the world knowing that the truth of my public journey is not only about overcoming nearly impossible odds, but about instilling hope to anyone suffering due to bipolar, directly or indirectly.

Sometimes referred to as manic-depressive illness, bipolar casts the inflicted individual's life into wild swings of highs and lows that often cause financial, emotional, and physical ruin. It is not just the individual that suffers. Their loved ones often watch with a feeling of hopelessness as their best efforts to support and help do little to avert the carnage bipolar leaves in its wake. Yet there is hope, there is *always* potential, and there are hidden strengths within the chaos and pain.

So why did I write this book and what can I offer that hasn't already been written? To be candid, I wasn't the one who wanted to write my memoir. My startling recovery was impactful enough that the very doctors that cared for me and watched my transformation asked me to write the memoir you are about to read. The purpose of sharing my journey was in hopes my recovery would startle the research community and help others understand a challenging diagnosis with more compassion, patience, and, most importantly, hope.

At first, I hesitated, and even resisted writing my story. However, the longer I remained stable, the better I was able to explain the intense and overwhelming swings in ways that helped others understand and cope with the diagnosis. With each passing day and week, a new and better way to explain bipolar and its complexity presented itself until I felt a duty to follow through on what was asked of me. When I felt I had truly refined my experiences to a degree that would help, I wrote my memoir.

I had no idea the repercussions writing my story would have on me personally. It takes but a few keystrokes to look me up on google, presenting liability concerns for the doctors that treat me, employers, and even romantic possibilities. Although I once saw this as a negative, I now realize that every time my recovery is questioned, my actions, my stability, and my very existence grants me the chance to open eyes to what we all need most in this world: hope.

Doubt is a normal reaction to what many might call and impossible recovery, and I fully admit I would doubt my own story had I not lived it. However, after proving myself time and since I first filed a provisional patent in 2009, I no longer need to explain myself. I show it each and every day with a calmness and stability I am proud of. Where I once felt insecure, I now love standing as a rare exception, astonishing some and leaving others waiting for me to falter.

The truth is, it has been over twelve years since I was officially, medically, declared in full remission of bipolar one. In that time, I have built a steady and successful business, helped many others recover utilizing the very treatment protocol that saved me, and I will continue to fight for each and every person who stumbles or is unable to articulate their struggles. My life is documented and I make it as public as possible. How else am I to stand and tell my story if I don't *live it* for all to see?

I still struggle, just as anyone does in this amazing journey we all share and face. I doubt, I fear, I stress just as anyone would. However, unlike someone without a diagnosis of bipolar, I am judged on a far more extreme scale. If sad, people that knew me before my recovery worry about suicide, while any happiness is seen as a warning sign for my loved ones, even after years without a single manic or hypomanic swing. All of this puts me in a position where I simply can't afford to fail, nor will I.

The cold hard truth is that many who suffer with bipolar are not even aware they are struggling. I had *no* idea the damage I was inflicting on myself and others, nor was I able to write with any depth or truth of what a bipolar "swing" felt like until I had been stable for a long while. Although it is a terrifying condition, it should never be seen as innately evil or bad. If someone were to give me the choice to go back in time and cure myself, I would promptly and vehemently decline. Although my life was a lesson in struggle, it was also a journey I needed to walk. One that led me to the man I am now proud to be. Who are we, really, without the struggles we overcome?

We all have regrets, or moments we wish we could alter, yet any removal of what sparked my creativity, drove my daring and often deadly risks, are the very same things that led me to stand up and proclaim to the world that I would not succumb to a label or fate not of my own making. Without bipolar, I wouldn't be changing the world for the better, nor helping anyone. The aforementioned statement goes for all psychiatric conditions. It is vital to understand that mental conditions are not 'illnesses' to fear, but unique minds that can be harnessed to create, build, and change the very reality we all share. It is time for us to see the beauty of our struggles instead of trying to erase them.

Although this book came out in 2013 and many were curious about the end results of my journey, I wanted to wait until I knew my stability could be sustained. As a dear friend and well known scientist, Richard Willams stated to me: "Anyone can find stability in short bursts, but to live it for years is proof of concept."

I am not someone special, I was simply blessed to be given a second chance. As you read my journey and the newly written epilogue, please remember that we are all deserving of a second chance. Moreover, we can attain it with enough grit, determination, and belief. There will always be stumbles, but that should never be enough to deter us from the dreams we desire to attain.

Life's journey may be brutal at times, yet I wouldn't change my struggles for anything in the world. It is in overcoming my trials that I found my heart, my purpose, and the will to be a better version of myself with each passing day. May my story inspire the same for you and your loved ones.

FOREWORD

:: Written By Dr. Dean Stull ::

Years ago I became a close friend to a young man who seemed "just" normal. I had known him since he was in elementary school and stayed in contact as he grew into a man. He struggled from time to time with what I thought was depression, but it seemed "manageable". He fell in love with a wonderful young woman. They were married and had two great little boys. I was suddenly introduced to reality when my friend was hospitalized in a catatonic state with a serious depression following an extreme manic period.

I visited him in the hospital and felt completely helpless; I can't imagine how his family felt. I learned that he had a long history of bipolar disorder that I had never suspected or even entertained as a possibility. Unfortunately, his family was not able to survive their bipolar ordeal, as they were never sure which person would be there on a given day.

Having been involved in the development of pharmaceuticals for most of my career, I looked into bipolar disorder to learn more about current treatment options, hoping to discover what I could do or advice I could offer to help my friend and his family. Almost all options seemed hopeless, and the treatments were very difficult for my friend, often providing no real help. I was confused and disturbed by how difficult this disorder is to identify and treat. I was further bothered by the lack of good pharmaceuticals for treatment.

Then I met Kirk Miller. He called me based upon a referral from a mutual friend. I was extremely skeptical, as my only point of reference with my friend and his constant battle with bipolar disorder. Kirk wanted my opinion of his personal experience with estrogen inhibitors and how they had helped him overcome his bipolar disorder. Kirk was interested in understanding what it would take to prove the benefit of using estrogen inhibitors in the treatment of bipolar sufferers and how he might best teach others about it.

Overtime, he earned my trust. I was impressed with his passion and persistence; he felt driven to give other sufferers their life back just as he had recovered his.

We spent time together talking about Kirk's experience and the results he and his doctor were seeing with other bipolar sufferers who are also trying estrogen inhibitors in their treatment. We also discussed ways to interest pharmaceutical companies and medical professionals in his experience and develop his treatment plan into a new and exciting option for doctors and future patients. In the end, we all agreed the telling Kirk's story to others was the best immediate option. I was impressed.

Most of us who have been impacted by or have a severe bipolar disorder (also known as manic-depressive disorder) know that over the past decade many books and articles have been published dealing with bipolar disorder. Physicians, psychiatrist, and other healthcare professionals have written important and detailed books defining and attempting to explain the condition. Others go into great detail describing historical and modern treatment strategies as well as ongoing research in clinical development. Current treatment strategies continue to be centered on drug cocktails, including mood stabilizers such as lithium, dissociative anesthetics, and dopamine agonists. Many books and articles address more non-traditional approaches, including diet changes, dietary supplements, extreme diets, and stress reduction techniques.

Unfortunately, many individuals suffering from bipolar disorder, like my friend, find little success from any of these approaches or are dissatisfied by the significant side effects when they reach a stable condition. Many of these individuals are willing to take extreme measures to improve their condition, knowing that they have been told that bipolar disorder is managed but never cured.

Parents, family members, and friends of individuals suffering from bipolar disorder have also written books. They provide insights into the disease, including its destructive impact on families, relationships, and individuals suffering from the condition. Bipolar suffers have also written about their past, navigating both the ups and the downs as well as exploring treatments for their condition. Some victims offer stories of survival and struggles in managing the condition.

Some of these books are positioned as self-help books, written in an effort to help suffers, family members, and friends cope with the condition and his destructive consequences. Although these books do offer comfort in just knowing that others have bipolar and are suffering, they do not really offer hope to the victims, their families, and their friends. Rather, the message all too often is about struggle and grief.

Chaos to Cured stands alone is a true, heartfelt telling of a dramatic realization that leads to a remarkable transformation sparked by determination and love. No one would ever want to live through the life experience described in this book; the details are just too hard. It's a story that in the end create a true sense of hope for bipolar sufferers.

As Kirk relives his story, the reader not only is captivated but immediately understands that this book is a true story written with the passion and truth only a bipolar sufferer could convey. Kirk's story includes some aspects of all the other stories, treatments, and self-help strategies. It is clear that the grip the disease has on individuals with bipolar disorder, their family, and their friends cannot be underestimated, overlooked, or dismissed.

Chaos to Cured tells a chilling story of the struggles of a bipolar sufferer, his family, and his friends; but at the end there is an unexpected surprise. There is love, there is hope, and there is a future.

Dean P. Stull, PhD
Friend, Scientist, Entrepreneur, and CEO

ACKNOWLEDGEMENTS

:: Special Thanks ::

-Dean P. Stull, PhD: There are no words for the support and kindness you have shown me as a mentor and a friend.

-Jeffrey Freed, author of *"Right Brained Child in a Left Brained World"*: Very few people saw my potential from the beginning. You did and continue to be a friend I'm blessed to have.

-Tiffany Werhner, LMHC: You believed in me and trusted me early on. I will continue to prove you correct, and so honored to know you.

-Dr. Denise McDermott: You change the world each day by helping others. It is an honor to know you and a blessing to call you a friend.

-Dr. Daniel LaPerriere: You treat me and everyone of your patients with respect. Not only are you a phenomenal MD, but a compassionate soul. Every MD should strive to be like you.

-John Poehler (The Bipolar Battle/author of *"This War Within my Mind"*): You are a dear friend who has walked much of the same path that I have, and continue to inspire others, including me.

-Richard R. Williams, PhD: A brilliant mind with an even bigger heart. Thank you for believing in me and pushing me onwards.

-Brent Meske: Simply the best editor on the planet. You're invaluable.

-To every person who has stood beside their children, siblings, and friends and loved them, even as they falter, this book and its epilogue are especially for you.

~Kirk Patrick Miller

PROFESSIONAL ENDORSEMENTS

:: Comments From Professionals ::

Here's what the experts who have read the book have to say.

Ø "Hope, strength, resiliency, and mental stability are words that come to mind in describing Author, Musician, Artist, and Athlete Kirk Patrick Miller. Kirk's ability to go into his suffering and alchemize his physical and mental life challenges to his unique thrive is Next Level Inspiring. This memoir is a reminder to 'Team Humanity' that all of the tools (Eastern, Western & Universal Ideology) in OUR toolbox allow us to HEAL at our own pace. Thank you Kirk for being a light for so many."
– Denise McDermott M.D., Paradigm Progression Pioneer, Integrative Adult and Child Psychiatrist

Ø "After practicing medicine for over forty years, I never dreamed that one of my patients would discover the most effective method of treating bipolar. Since dealing with Kirk Miller, we still do not know if it is a complete cure or the treatment has kept his bipolar is in a constant state of remission, however, the results I have seen with Mr. Miller and the others who have undergone the same treatment are undeniable. I hope everyone will find Mr. Miller's memoir as inspiring and surprising as I found watching his recovery. I feel lucky to have been a part of a once in a lifetime discovery."

– Dr. Robert Simon, M.D.

Ø "Kirk Miller's memoir provides important, if not vital, insight into the bipolar condition. After working with over two thousand different individuals throughout the world, all suffering from ADD, dyslexia, and bipolar syndrome I can say, without reserve, that seldom, if ever, have I read such an in-depth and fascinating account of what it is like to be truly bipolar. The fact that the author has cured himself and discovered a potential cure has revolutionary implications. Kirk Miller needs to be heard and heard widely. I endorse his memoir with overwhelming enthusiasm."

– Jeffery Freed, M.A.T., Author of *Right-Brained Children in a Left-Brained World*

Ø "Here is a book, which I believe is one of a kind...The in-depth story this Mr. Miller shares is a rare look in to the mind of a bipolar episode...I believe that Mr. Miller has indeed found a way out of the emotional and mental prison in which bipolar has incarcerated so many individuals. I would encourage anyone and everyone to read this memoir, especially if you know someone with bipolar."

– Debra Slackman, MA, Clinical Psychotherapist

Ø "Mr. Miller provides a unique insight into the inner workings of a Bipolar person's heart and mind, from the perspective of someone who has experienced it before and after successful treatment. This book is a must-have resource for anyone who loves a Bipolar person—but has a hard time understanding how Bipolar Disorder affects his/her thinking, mood, and actions."

– Sheryl Gurrentz, Co-Author of *If Your Child is Bipolar: A Parent-to-Parent Guide to Living with and Loving a Bipolar Child*

TABLE OF CONTENTS

PART ONE: FLYING TOO CLOSE TO THE SUN

:: Mania's Flight Before the Fall Into Darkness ::

I. FLIGHT OF ICARUS

The moonlight sliced into the alleyway, its sharp lines creating a beautiful contrast between everything it touched and the black shadows that I lay in. I forced my aching eyes open and stared up at the night sky, blinking as my eyes adjusted to the streetlamps. The stars were lost to the city lights, but the moon was full and bright, its cool blue hue making the alleyway seem cold.

My head throbbed and the world spun gently when I tried to move. The cold, hard cement I was lying upon felt oddly soothing as my heart pounded. Drenched in sweat, I contemplated lying there, but I couldn't remain still. Even with the extreme quantity of alcohol and drugs flowing through my veins, my mind continued to race, jumping from one thought to another with no clear rhyme or reason. I simply couldn't remain in place.

I was twenty-one at the time and even though I was still drunk and high, I was aching to silence my mind. I wanted more of everything, unaware that none would help. It would be another year until I was told that those racing thoughts and inability to quiet my mind were related to what professionals called a manic episode. I was self-medicating in an attempt to slow the world down around me, but it wasn't working, nor had it ever worked.

This was not the first time that a mixture of drugs and alcohol had left me passed out in a less than ideal location. I had woken up in worse and far more dangerous situations, yet I never thought anything about it, nor cared. To me, the world always found a way to punish me, so why would I care where I awoke? Not once, regardless of how bad things might have appeared to others, did it occur to me that my actions were not those of a 'normal' mind, especially when I was simply desperate to calm the unrelenting torrent of racing thoughts rushing through my mind.

As was often the case when I awoke from a drug binge, everything felt louder and brighter. Yet even as the streetlamps stung my dilated eyes, I felt powerful, unstoppable, and I had no ability to stay focused. All I wanted to do was release the energy continuing to expand within me and I wasn't going to get it done while lying in the alleyway.

Although I was now of legal drinking age, legality had never been an issue to me. I had a secret history of using and selling harder drugs. Due to the paranoia that was constantly tainting my thoughts, I kept such parts of my life extremely quiet and hidden even from my closest friends. At the time, I had no knowledge that much of my substance use was due to a need for self-medication. I was absolutely unaware that, as my mania grew more intense, so did my desire for more extreme drugs and risks.

As I rubbed my eyes, a dry smile formed upon my lips as my mind obsessed on what drug or experience would excite me enough to overpower the intensity of the night, moment, and world around me. Thoughts of drugs and alcohol flooded my mind as was often the case. I had never taken any drug seriously. When I was as amped as I was, it didn't matter what chemical I used or what form of delivery was utilized. Only one thing mattered: filling my body with enough of something that would take me away from my own mind.

At the time, I had the potential to be a good person, but something had always steered me away from warmth and kindness. I was a selfish individual. I wouldn't allow my sister to sing because I had absolute pitch and any missed note was like fingers on a chalkboard. I refused to share, mostly because I trusted no one. Even when it came to food, I would protect it as if everyone else was plotting on eating what I viewed as mine. My view of life was seen through a warped lens. I didn't see good in others, but only darkness and danger. So, in some ways, it is not surprising that I chose to be selfish. If everyone was out to take advantage of me, why wouldn't I choose to protect myself?

I could be nice, but only if it held the chance to benefit me. If I knew that being polite might gain me special benefits, I could instantly turn on my charm. I didn't see it as manipulation, but instead as a tool for self-preservation. Just as I was able to utilize kindness, I could also be extremely cruel. When challenged or feeling threatened, I had the ability to pick out someone's deepest insecurity and use it to harm them when I felt threatened. At the time, I had no idea I did these things. So much of it came naturally and without effort, but it also came at a heavy cost. The reason I was able to read others was because I viewed every encounter as a threat. In short, I was lost to my own reality. That distorted and sad reality left me isolated, uncaring about myself, my future. I certainly wasn't going to care for others if I didn't value my own existence.

Unable to remain still any longer, I groaned as I moved. Getting up and off my back took far more effort than I had expected. It certainly wasn't helped by the spinning world that made me feel as if I would fall over without complete focus. Slowly I rolled over to my front and pushed myself up until I was resting upon my knees. Leaning back and taking a long breath of the cool night air, my smile never faded.

The moment would have been perfect for self-examination, but at the time I didn't think twice. In fact I never did. To me, I was doing great and my instincts were, incorrectly, perceived as flawless. My grades in college were good, I had quite a few romantic relationships that were flourishing, and I was working on what I thought was a groundbreaking fiction manuscript that would bring me fame and fortune. I had no doubt of my own brilliance and there wasn't anything on the planet that was going to keep me down.

Ready to find my next rush, I felt my smile expand as my eyes glistened with a danger and wildness I was oblivious to. Placing my closed fists against the ground, unaware of the pebbles and dirt cutting into my knuckles, I pushed myself up. As I rose to my feet, I nearly stumbled until I used the brick wall beside me to keep the spinning world from throwing me back to the ground.

After catching myself, I suddenly noticed that my right sleeve was torn. I had a deep scratch on my forearm that had bled and stained one of my favorite shirts. I touched the wound with my other hand, running my fingertips along the rough surface of the dried blood. A normal person might have paused to think how they had ended up passed out in an alleyway, their shirt torn and their right arm wounded. I wasn't close to normal and my racing mind had deeper concerns. Therefore, I simply shrugged and walked out of the shadows ready to enjoy what was left of the waning night.

I tried to get my bearings at the end of the alleyway. The streets were empty except for a few homeless individuals wrapped in sheets and newspapers to protect them from the slight breeze that had picked up. I wasn't in the best section of Denver's downtown and although I remembered entering one of the more popular clubs with my friends, as well as drinking, I couldn't remember how or why I had wandered so far from the main strip of bars and clubs. I was never one to wonder what had transpired, so instead I started walking towards the only main street I recognized. The night was fading but I was hell bent on getting my fill of fun.

After walking for a few blocks, I heard my friend. "Kirk, I've been looking all over for you!" Mike's face was hard and filled with a mixture of relief and frustration. He came running to catch up with me.

"What's wrong?"

Mike just stood there for a moment, staring at me, most likely equal parts frustration and amazement. "What's wrong? Really?"

I could tell he was a bit upset but I headed past him and towards the stoplight. Mike continued to talk while rushing to catch up on our way to our unstoppable, inevitable great time. "Man, what the hell happened back there? That stunt you pulled back at the bar got the cops involved. I barely made it out before they arrived. Why the hell did you throw that mug at the bouncer?"

The memory came flooding back, and I remembered meeting up with a girl and buying her a drink when I had thought I overheard the people sitting next to us talking about me. I could still remember feeling their eyes on me, staring and judging. It had ticked me off and like every decision in my life, I didn't think. Instead I lashed out.

I couldn't recall everything that had happened. I did remember approaching the men at the next table and pushing the first one that met my gaze. A small skirmish had broken out and although someone had tried to break it up, I had already gotten hold of a beer mug, only to chuck it across the bar. It missed the bartender by a few inches. When the glass shattered against the wall and the bouncers and staff began to make their way over toward me, I remembered wanting to fight. Luckily, Mike had taken hold of me and pushed me towards the door, telling me to run. As everyone began to close in on me, I felt certain everyone in the club was out to get me and I wasn't about to be captured. I pushed my way through the stunned crowd squeezed out the door.

I couldn't help but chuckle at the memory, which Mike did not appreciate. He shoved me half-heartedly. "Seriously, dude, you could've gotten me busted, especially with the crap I'm holding for you."

When Mike pushed me, I could feel my temper flare up and I almost lashed out, but I was more interested in getting back to the clubs. "Let's forget it and have some fun."

Mike shook his head. "You can't go back there, bro. Plus, it's three in the morning and the clubs are closed."

"That doesn't mean we can't have some fun," I responded lightly, with mischief. Mike's serious face softened. When I wanted to be charming, I was very good at it and Mike responded, laughing lightly as he looked at my shirt.

Mike was no stranger to trouble, and I think he found my sudden explosions entertaining. "If that sleeve hadn't ripped, you'd be sitting in jail right now. You should make that your lucky shirt."

I didn't wonder how it had happened; I never did. I'd ended up a mile or more away from the clubs somehow. Instead of wondering what had happened, why I had felt so paranoid or why I had lashed out so violently, all I could focus on was how to extend the evening. I was more eager than ever to enjoy the rest of the night. I may have been drunk and drugged, but that didn't change the fact that I felt an immense amount of energy that I was itching to burn off. When Mike suggested we head to an after-hours club, I agreed.

When alcohol stopped being served, the night scene didn't vanish, but merely changed. The after-hour clubs were a place for drugs and a more extreme idea of partying, though they tried to police their establishments.

"Let's go." Mike smiled and slugged me in the arm, his way of showing me all was forgiven.

Mike was a great guy and partied with me more than any of my other friends. This was mostly because he found me entertaining, but it was also due to the fact that his drug and alcohol problems made him less sensitive to my sudden outbursts and explosions. I didn't know it at the time, but my erratic behavior had already begun to terrify my family and closest friends. In many ways, Mike was my party friend, not really connected to me in any other way or through other friends. At times, however, my sudden violence would even catch Mike off guard, but only at my most extreme. It would be years later that Mike would vanish, lost to the drugs he always longed for.

After spending three more hours at an after-hours club, the sun was up, and Mike was worn down. I was sober now but still aching for more action. My mind was continuing to ricochet from one thought to another at unbelievable speeds, and I was having a hard time concentrating. We had run out of drugs, so we called it a night. Mike couldn't keep up with me. Even despite my objections, he talked me into heading home.

The drive home was quick, and I was enjoying the feel of his car on the highway. "Dude, you gotta' slow down and would you please stop talking. My head is killing me."

Mike's hangover had finally caught up to him and apparently I was loud. I cranked up the radio instead, and pushed the accelerator down, unaware that he had even asked me to slow my speed. Although the car was speeding past ninety miles an hour, everything felt so slow. I heard Mike ask for me to slow down again, but I couldn't. Mike saw the danger in my driving and speed, but my reality was of every other car on the road moving at a snail's pace and it actually angered me. Mike sighed, knowing me well enough to understand that I wasn't going to listen.

When we arrived at my home, it was seven in the morning and I wasn't the least bit tired. "How about doing something tonight?"

Mike just looked over at me like I was crazy. "We'll see. Right now, I need to get some sleep. I'll call you soon, though."

I got out, all nerves and energy as Mike slid over the emergency brake and into the driver's seat. Standing with the driver's door open I drummed impatiently on the roof of his car as my foot tapped faster the longer I waited for him to finally get into the driver's seat. "You just remember to call. I have nothing to do and it'll be fun."

"It's always an adventure," Mike said, a hint of a laugh in his voice. I stepped back, closed his door and watched as he drove out of the cul-de-sac and vanished from view. Still tapping my foot with what felt like endless energy, I paced in the driveway as the rest of the neighbors slept. I didn't want to sleep, but it was too early for anything that I wanted to do. What had started at the beginning of the evening as raw energy was slowly transforming into anger and rage that I was unaware of.

Walking into my house, I contemplated calling an acquaintance that was always up for a party. Considering the time, I figured they wouldn't answer, so I proceeded into the basement and down to my room. Still unable to quiet my mind or the growing rage that was building up, I opened my dresser and reached towards the back.

Grasping a sock stuffed with drugs, I pulled it out and dumped the contents onto the top of the dresser. Sprawled across the top was a variety of narcotics I should not have possessed. I never thought of consequences, especially in such agitated states. There were a few small bags of cocaine, but the last thing I wanted was anything to speed my mind. The downers also didn't interest me. Alcohol hadn't worked, so I knew the hard pills I had wouldn't work. So I reached for a sheet of paper. Although some of my friends knew about LSD, few knew that I dipped my own sheets. I knew I could sell the small squares I cut from the sheets at an astronomical profit, but the truth was I couldn't stick with anything, certainly not dealing.

Breaking off a small square and placing it under my tongue, I grabbed a pair of earphones and plugged them into my CD Walkman. I didn't even look to see what CD was in the player as I fell back onto my bed, turning up the volume to dangerous levels for my ears. Closing my eyes, I couldn't help but feel a heat within, and also looming danger. Even in my own room, my mind continued to race and grow more restless. Lying upon the bed, I wasn't even aware my hands were balled into tight fists as the LSD began to make my skin tingle as patterns formed on the back of my eyelids. After what felt like an eternity of trying to quiet my thoughts, I knew I couldn't sleep. Giving up, I stood up and walked out the basement door. If I couldn't sleep, perhaps the rising sun, LSD and music would drown out my thoughts.

What I didn't know at the time was that my manic episodes were not a single stage event. They started off slowly and continued to build. They always started off with a sudden spike of energy and productivity. My mind would then race faster and unabated until I reached the second stage in which my focus was lost and all I wanted to do was slow it down. As the music blared, I could feel the energy and fight within giving way to what I can only describe as a peak.

Although I didn't know it at the time, my final stage and peak was always accompanied by delusions. I would honestly believe I was smarter and stronger than others, as well as capable of seeing things others couldn't. This was always accompanied by paranoia. It was a dangerous mixture of thoughts. Not only did I feel invincible, but as paranoia became more prominent within my mind, I would see others as trying to steal my ideas or conspiring against me. It led me to self-isolation, removed my ability to trust, and also created a dangerous mindset that I could either strike first or become a victim.

The mixture of feeling invincible while also sensing that everyone was out to get me made me dangerous. There is no other way to state it. I was a risk to myself, my family, friends, and anyone that I might misperceive as trying to cause me harm. This mindset also led to more fights that I care to recall. Luckily, I had never been seriously injured, although I had taken quite a few beatings. What I had done to others is still unknown to me, but my friends always pulled me off and away before I could seriously harm someone.

Although much of the most inspired, productive, and creative moments in my life came when I was at the first stage of my mania, the price I paid for those flashes of brilliance was never worth the cost. My manic peaks would end with a terrifying eruption of violence and anger that made me a danger to myself and everyone around me. I wouldn't know until years later that that peak was a warning that I was about to crash into a deep depression. It never failed. The higher and more intense the peak, the quicker and more violent the fall into darkness.

II. FLYING HIGH ON WINGS OF WAX

As I stood in the driveway the sun continued to rise above the Denver skyline, beginning to cast its warm glow onto our small street and my mother's garden. I didn't mind living at home, but that evaporated when I entered the house to find my mother and father standing in the kitchen staring at me. Their worry was etched on their faces, from the deep circles beneath their eyes, but that quickly melted into anger. Of course, I thought, they'd jump straight into judging me. I became defensive and prepared for a fight. Anyone who knows my parents would know that they only care. They are both gentle and kind people, but they were growing tired of my radical emotions. My mother and sister, in particular, were tired of feeling like they had to walk and talk cautiously so as not to upset me. They had every right.

"Where have you been?" My mother spoke first, adding, "I've been worried sick. The least you could've done was call." I never knew, or it never truly sank in, but my family had always worried about me when I went out. Unlike the people who knew me only as a friend, only those that lived with me saw the truth of my mental problems and knew how violent and irrational I could become.

I didn't care about my mother's concern as my mania had taken over and was worsening. I lashed out, my voice booming and filled with anger. "I'm twenty-one years old, Mom. You can cut the parent crap." My tone must have been harsher and louder than I thought because my mother took a step back, a bit of surprise edging out the anger on her face as my dad stood up and stepped between us.

My dad is one of the most gentle and easy-going people on the planet, but even he looked a bit irritated. "That's no way to talk to your mother."

I was taller and more muscular than my father and instead of talking, I walked past, slamming my shoulder into his in an act that still repulses me. I was not in my right mind and I saw everyone as my enemy. I used more force than I'd intended, but it didn't matter at that point. There was no regret, and certainly no remorse. Instead I shouted at them as I walked towards the basement door. "Lay off, I was out with friends."

I had been in a great mood, but my jubilation caused by the excitement of the previous night had quickly transformed to an anger that I couldn't shake. My parents stood quietly, watching me walk away and down into my basement room. As a final show of my anger, I slammed the door as hard as I could. It splintered, and a section of it broke away. Too angry to go to bed, I walked into the larger portion of the basement where all of my painting supplies were stored. My thoughts were still all over the place.

I decided I would paint.

Handling my mania was like walking on a razor's edge. I didn't understand anything about my mind or what was wrong at the time, nor did I realize that I was becoming more dangerous, angry, violent, paranoid and delusional. With no ability to analyze myself, I was trapped between euphoria and utter despair. The only thing keeping my mind from crashing was the paint that I was hastily and violently stroking onto the canvas.

I had no way of knowing that my mania was going to grow more intense and would eventually peak. I didn't even know what mania was. It is easy now to understand that the first stage of my mania made me witty, playful and confident. My thoughts came fast and easy. I loved those moments as I was always productive and going out with my usual friends was extremely fun. The creativity and ideas that came to me during that first stage was amazing, but it quickly spiraled out of control.

The second stage was an amplification of the first, only my ability to focus was lost and I was unable to concentrate or finish the many projects I had started. Also, my wit would become edgy while my view of the world and my place in it would border on delusional. Typically, it was during the second stage that I would go out drinking and seeking any and all drugs in an attempt to calm and quiet the whirlwind my mind became.

Currently, my second stage was quickly speeding out of control. Even as I painted, I couldn't shake my anger. Anger, aggressiveness and frustration with everything around me was a clue that I was about to begin hitting my peak. The people I cared about were the first to end up in the crosshairs. The peak was always violent and filled with anger at the world and everyone in it. On rare occasions, I would even believe I was meant for something more, believing that I was better than those around me. This feeling would always lead me to wonder why I wasn't already famous and why the world plotted against me. It was this final peak that caused damage to both my personal and professional relationships and always set me back.

Unaware that my coming mental state always caused me to lose opportunities and destroy friendships, I painted faster. No sleeping, no eating, no talking, just painting. After six straight hours of nonstop painting I had run out of canvases. I had painted four large landscapes and I can see now that the brush strokes were crude and brash, just like my mind, but they weren't bad.

I was certain then I'd end up rich and famous. These were clearly masterpieces. My book was going to be a bestseller and my paintings would make me millions, not to mention that I had figured out the secret to trading stocks. I certainly was beyond anything that I could learn at a college or job. I was mistaken.

Some thumping upstairs and muffled voices announced that my sister was home. . This was perfect. I hadn't gotten anything for my sister's birthday and what could be better than an original painting by her soon-to-be famous brother. When I got upstairs, I presented the painting to my family. Like always, everyone wasn't sure what mood I would be in, but they were glad that I was not shouting. Before my sister saw the painting, I could see that she had heard that I had gotten back late and had worried my parents, but she quickly averted her gaze and focused on the painting. Everyone loved what I had painted for my sister, but I could sense that they were still upset.

"Kirk," she said cautiously and quietly, as if she wasn't sure she should say anything. Slowly, she pointed to my cargo shorts and the streaks of paint that stained them. "Your favorite shorts. Why don't we get those into the wash..." I had forgotten to change before painting, but my sister's voice trailed off as I looked down at the stains. It was such a small thing, but apparently my sister and parents could see the impending explosion and all three took a step back.

She was right. Oil paints were smeared on my shorts. All positive feelings I might have felt were swept away and my mania entered the third and most volatile stage. At first my voice was quiet, although my knuckles were turning white as I gripped the edge of the painting. "Son of a," I didn't finish my statement. Instead I turned and punched the door to the basement as hard as I could. Although the door wasn't solid core, it didn't break with the first hit, but instead cracked down the middle. The violence and suddenness of my action made my family jump and I noticed my sister jerk back in surprise. I was overcome with anger. My favorite shorts were ruined. I made sure to swing harder this time, and the door was no match for my fury. My hand went through it. I don't remember gasps of horror, the crunch of wood or the pain, but my sister tried to calm me down next.

"Kirken," my sister said gently, always the peacekeeper. It was a burden she should never have had to carry and caused her more grief than such a sweet woman ever deserved. "I'm sure Mom can get the stains out."

"No!" The volume and aggression in my voice took everyone aback and I could feel my mind spinning out of control as the rage I felt, baseless as it was, blinded me to the reality I was seeing. Everyone, my parents, sister, friends and the world seemed against me and I just wanted to pound my fist repeatedly into something. I took hold of my shorts and pointed to the stains as if my sister couldn't see them. "This is oil paint and it's been sitting on my shorts for hours! They're ruined!" I tore off my shorts and stripped down to my boxers in a rage. I began to curse and slam my hand and fist into anything close. After leaving multiple holes in the drywall as I walked out to the garage. My mom and sister were crying, and I could hear my dad shouting that I needed to calm down, but his voice was distant, overrun by the river of rage that was flooding my every fiber.

As I left the kitchen and walked into the garage wearing only my dirty shirt from the night before and my boxers, I could hear my family arguing behind me as to what to do. My father didn't understand my actions, my mom was crying and shouting back at my father, and my sister tried to calm them down. All this happened while she was holding a four-foot long painting that she had caught when I dropped it, trying to keep the paint from staining the carpet.

I had the keys to my car, but I couldn't think of anywhere I wanted to go, so I stalked down my driveway. I was far too angry to calm down. I wanted to hurt something, and perhaps myself. The mailbox, unfortunately, was the last thing to feel my wrath. I slammed my fist into it again and again until it flew off its post. My shirt was now stained with my own blood; my knuckles had been broken open from all my lashing out

When my sister came out to try and calm me down, she paused at the door, her eyes wide with surprise and horror at the scene before her. As I had gone through the garage, I had broken a rake, some pieces of scrap wood, the garage door opener, and all before tipping over a file cabinet. I wonder now what my sister thought as she stared past my swath of destruction, watching me kick the mailbox post with my bare shins and feet. "Stop it!"

My sister's pleading was of no use and I was beyond words. I was lashing out at the world that refused to give me what I deserved while ruining everything I loved. I hadn't realized that my storm of curse words and actions had drawn the neighbors of our quiet cul-de-sac to their doors. They watched as though I were a rabid dog or a house fire. I think it was more out of fear that no one called the police. I couldn't be contained or calmed, and I hate to think what I might have done had the police shown up to detain me. Contemplating my state of mind, I expect I would've ended up in jail, which is a place I should've been sent many times throughout my life.

My sister walked towards me, gently calling out my name and telling me I was making a scene. I finally noticed all the eyes that were staring at me. They were all judging me, their watchful and accusing eyes making me realize that I had to get away.

I had to get away. I sped past my sister, who was cautiously standing back and still, her face filled with worry and confusion, I got into my car and started the engine. After some angry revving, my mom and dad emerged, pleading with me to calm down. Music as loud as it would go, seething, I slammed the stick shift into reverse and backed out of the driveway without even checking if my sister or anyone else was behind me.

My tires squealed as I flew through the gentle neighborhood. I floored it, and I remember wondering: *Why am I even here?* At that moment, I truly hated myself and the world. The bright future my mania had enabled me to see now felt like a lie. I was useless, unable to even paint without ruining something I cared about. Seeping in self-pity, I couldn't see beyond myself. I didn't worry about my family or how I had verbally attacked the very people that loved me. I didn't worry about the damage to property, or even myself. I might have broken my hand, and maybe my foot.

Like Icarus I'd gotten too close to the sun, and my wings had melted. The inevitable fall from a great height would be swift. And like gravity, it could not be stopped.

Eventually, I slowed down and pulled off to the side of the road, not because I wanted to, but because my brain was shutting down. I felt confused and the colors around me seemed dull and gray like the fog of depression that was quickly overtaking me. The anger that had been fueling me had vanished, leaving me on the side of the road with no idea why I deserved such a fate while wondering if I should simply drive off a cliff and end my suffering.

With the emergency brake engaged and the car in neutral I rested my forehead on the steering wheel. I wanted to shout out or cry, but I had stopped crying by the time I was in third grade. The mania that had been protecting me from the pain that was now throbbing from my bloody and swollen knuckles and bare feet was gone, but the physical pain was nothing compared to mental anguish that had suddenly cast a shadow over my entire world view. The feeling that I was capable of anything and meant for great things had, in a single instant, vanished, leaving me feeling vulnerable, helpless, hopeless and pathetic.

I truly wasn't aware that anything out of the ordinary had happened. To me, it didn't seem odd to be on the top of the world one minute and wishing for death the next. The truth, however, was that once again the blissful razor of mania had again grown too sharp to keep my footing. Looking back, I shudder when remembering how it felt to plummet into despair.

III. PLUMMET

Depression had taken hold. I sat in the car for a long time, my body weighted down by some unknown force, and my lips tightened as I tried hard to breathe, but I felt like a heavy blanket had been draped over me and not only was it hard to breathe, I wasn't sure if I cared. With my head and hands resting on the steering wheel and dressed only in a T-shirt and boxers, I didn't care about anything.

The radio was on, but the music sounded distant while my throbbing hands and feet seemed disconnected. I wasn't aware of the damage I had caused, nor could I feel any pain. The darkness that was draped over my mind dulled everything and distorted time. Without any place to go and nowhere I desired to be, I just sat there, unmoving and uncaring. At the moment, I wondered what it would be like if I simply fell asleep and never woke up. My mania had peaked, and I had crashed down into a pool of self-loathing. Although I had been a completely different person during the previous three weeks as my mania had been ramping up, I didn't know anything was wrong. The inability to understand reality would become worse over the years, but I didn't know it at the time.

Looking back, it is clear that I had been overcome with a heavy depression, but at the time, I didn't even know or care that I had been a completely different person only hours ago. To change so drastically was something I should have noticed, but my mind was simply unaware of anything but what I was feeling at the moment. In fact, everything good that had ever happened to me seemed like a façade. It was as if someone had tricked me into believing in happiness.

I tried to reach forward to turn off the blaring music and was surprised at how hard such a simple motion was. My arm felt heavy and the desire to move simply wasn't strong enough, so I left the radio on. The music stopped and advertisements blared out of the speakers. I couldn't even reach the radio controls. I wondered if life was a waste and if everything I believed would bring me happiness was worth the effort. I felt like giving up.

Tired of everything, including my life, I wanted to shout towards the heavens and curse whatever force had brought me into existence, but even the idea of shouting seemed overwhelming. I should've been surprised when I heard someone tapping on my window, but I didn't even move my head.

When my door was opened from the outside and I felt a hand gently touch my shoulder, I didn't even move. Had it been a few hours earlier, I might have snapped, but under the crushing weight of depression I was devoid of energy and didn't want to open my eyes. When my sister spoke, her voice seemed distant, yet gentle. "Are you hurt? Did something happen?"

I didn't answer.

"I'm going to take you home, okay?" It was both asking for permission and a statement. She took hold of my left arm and gently pulled, trying to help me out of the driver's seat. My body felt thick and sludgy, and although I didn't want to see or talk to anyone, I didn't have the energy to fight, so I let my sister guide me around the back of the car and into the passenger's seat. I plopped down in the seat but didn't even reach out to close the door.

"Can you get the door?" she asked, before walking away. Her voice was laced with frustration, but mostly concern. When I still didn't move, she made sure the door wouldn't hit me and closed it before walking around to the driver's side.

After the door shut, I leaned my head against the cool glass, staring into the rearview mirror and recognizing my father's headlights. As always, I was lost in my own reality, feeling unloved by the world and the people close to me. Even as I was being taken care of, I was unable to connect that my family had cared enough to come looking for me. With my mind quickly shutting down, I was unable to see the truth that my family loved me and had always put up with more than they deserved. To this day, I still feel pangs of guilt knowing the pain I caused my family. I was loved, but despair overwhelmed me, and I felt alone and lost.

When my sister got into the car, she turned off the stereo and pointed to my seatbelt. "Put your seatbelt on." She was so patient with me. But of course I didn't move, keeping my head leaning against the window. My mind was so foggy I had heard her suggestion but couldn't respond. Like the amazing sister she was, Chandi reached over, took hold of my seatbelt and buckled me in. After clicking me safely into place, my sister continued to talk. "Did you hit something? Why were you just sitting there on the side of the road?"

For the first time I spoke. "Does it really matter?" I responded, my voice flat and hollow.

"Of course it does," my sister said gently. Her attempt to soothe me went unheard. I didn't notice as I was unable to think of anything other than how horrible my life was, when in reality, I was very blessed and loved. "What were you thinking?" Chandi asked. She then sighed and added, "You realize you owe everyone an apology. You had everyone worried sick and you certainly did a good job getting the neighbors' attention."

"Like it matters," was all I could say. "I just want to sleep." The statement was only half true. I did want to sleep, but I didn't want to wake up to the world that had turned on me and felt so strange and bleak.

Like much of my past, I wasn't aware of what was happening, and it is only now that I know that my mind had shut down, the mania had vanished from beneath my feet and left me to fall into the beginning of my depressive phase. Much like my mania, my depression also had different stages. The first was always the same and, most of the time, followed my manic peaks. Like I felt in the car, my first stage of depression would make my mind feel sluggish and I was always left with the feeling that everything I had been working for was either slipping away or was already gone. It was also a time when I stayed away from my friends and family, even though I needed them more then than ever. Unable to express that I just needed to be near someone who cared about me, mixed with my instinct to pull away from everything and everyone I cared about did not help my downs.

Although I would be considered dangerous to myself and others, the people that knew me only saw or dealt with me in my first stage of my mania, masking my mental problems. Most of closest friends and relatives had no idea how much I was suffering while those unlucky enough to live with me saw the darkest sides of my swings.

When I was younger, both my mania and depression had been less severe, making those that questioned my actions blame my swings on the hormones of a simple teenager. As the years went by, however, my moods became more severe and disruptive. It had been a gradual process, each swing getting worse and then I hit my twenties. I have to be clear that I had always been out of control; even as a child my reactions were out of touch with reality. Drugs and alcohol didn't help, but they certainly didn't cause the bipolar that plagued me. As I grew older, however, my swings began to worry my family as they disrupted not only every aspect of my own life, but took a heavy and devastating toll on those dearest to me.

When we arrived home, I got out of the car and before anyone could speak to me. I couldn't bear to be interrogated. I used all of my energy to push open my door, standing up and walking into the house with my head down, my boxers twisted and my shoulders slumped forward. As much as I needed support, I wasn't mentally capable of receiving it and headed into my basement. I closed the door I'd broken and collapsed on my bed.

Even with my eyes closed, I was unable to escape the feeling that I was trapped by some unseen force. Like a heavy weight pressing down on my chest, my breathing was shallow, my eyes were sensitive, and I welcomed death. Make no mistake, I never wanted to feel so depressed, but the harder I tried to climb out of the depression that had overtaken me, the tighter the cage that held me in darkness became.

I just need to sleep, I remember thinking, completely unaware that the anguish I felt was only the beginning stage of my depressive swing. The depression wasn't going anywhere.

IV. DEEPENING

I awoke the next day feeling no different than the night before. Not only did I not want to get up, I hated the fact that I had awakened. All I wanted was to sleep, but my depression was still in the first stage and I was slightly hungry and, since I hadn't showered in two days, I smelled.

Getting out of bed took nearly an hour and more energy than I thought I could muster. Unable to hold a steady job or stay in college, I remember focusing on how messed up the world was. I hated the idea that every day felt the same as I struggled to gain a foothold on my dreams. When I analyze myself now, I can't help but see that I was always focused on dreams and not my future. Everything was based on the present, with no ability to sense or fear my past or future, making my depressions torturous. The inability to see beyond the moment might be considered a good thing to some, but without reality to ground me, it was beyond a hindrance.

I know now that having even a slight grasp of what I wanted in the future would've helped guide my present, but my logical skills were lost in depression and tainted to an extreme during my manic episodes. Although I had dreams like anyone else, my inability to focus on how to reach my lofty goals only made me miss out on the steps I needed to take in order to make my dreams and goals a reality. If I could go back, I would not have neglected my studies as I was caught up in the belief that I was too smart and too important for school or work. Of course, that day, my depression made my goals feel impossible, nor did I really care if I reached them or not.

I just sat on the bathroom floor, wondering why I had to suffer. What god would cause such pain and what had I done to deserve such a fate? Of course, my lack of understanding anything but the present led to rash and illogical actions that often led me further away from the things I most cared about. Also, because all my decisions were made based on what I was feeling at that very instant, my actions cost me relationships, friendships and countless job opportunities.

Eventually I stood up and walked back to my room. It was summer break, not that it mattered. College had already proven too steady and regimented for me to handle, so I had fallen back on the only skill I had, playing the violin. You see, I'd seen a rainbow, which was clearly a sign that I should follow my dreams of writing, painting and fame. Therefore I'd given up my full ride scholarship at the university of Denver.

Now skill was all I had. Luckily, I only had a few students and they only saw me when I was functioning in the first stage of my mania. At those times, I was great at reading my students and guiding them, though I wasn't steady enough to be a great teacher. I'd cancel for weeks at a time when depressed or simply miss the lessons when I was manic. Due to my current mental state, I knew I wouldn't be able to teach, but neither did I want to use the phone to cancel.

I stood up with a great deal of effort and entered my small basement shower, ignoring, almost welcoming the pain that was caused when the water slammed into the cut on my arm and my bruised and beaten feet and knuckles. I deserved to feel pain as I knew I was useless. My gaze then fell upon the razor in the shower. I knew how to properly cut my veins to ensure a quick death. With razor in hand, I just stared at the sparkling blades, wondering if I should end it all.

A deep, drawn out sigh escaped me. I didn't even have the drive to shave or soap my body down, let alone end my life. I made the supreme effort of putting the razor back before I turned off the water. For any number of minutes I simply stood there and let the water slide down my body. Eventually I walked out of the shower and into my room.

On my dresser was a napkin from the previous night with a woman's phone number written in blue ink. Next to the note was a new pair of the same shorts I had ruined the night before, but I didn't even care that my mom had not only taken the time to find another pair but spent her own money in an attempt to cheer me up. The idea of calling anyone sounded like torture so I crawled into bed, not even bothering to dry or dress myself.

As I closed my eyes, I knew that I wanted nothing to do with anything, anyone or the world. I wasn't happy, but every time I thought of something that might make me feel better, my chest tightened, and I felt another smothering wave of sadness that kept my mind from even thinking about anything pleasurable. *This isn't what life is supposed to be,* I thought as I fell asleep, unaware that a few tears had fallen out of the corner of my eyes, rolling down my chin and falling to my pillow.

V. TWILIGHT DAYS

I didn't improve over the next two weeks and every day was a struggle just to keep moving. I didn't understand why I even tried to shower or eat as the only time I felt any break from a feeling of worthlessness was when I slept. I had been able to teach, since I only had three students at the time, all of whom I liked, but with each passing day everything became more strenuous and stressful.

My family tried to help, but whenever my mother, father or sister talked to me the conversations were brief and I was easily agitated, making my family feel tense and worried. It was clear that my mother and sister were trying to cheer me up, but whenever they tried, I turned cold and quickly retreated to my room. I wanted to feel better, but had no way of climbing out of the hole I was in. Worst of all, I was completely unaware that anything was wrong with me. In my opinion, it was the world that was tainted, and I wanted no part. In many ways, this lack of reality protected me from seeing the truth, for had I been aware of all the relationships I had ruined while also being depressed, I have no doubt that I would've taken my own life. Eventually the number of edges I'd find in this double-edged sword would astonish me.

Although I had somehow survived for two weeks, I still felt no relief and each day felt worse and darker than the previous one. The only thing that was changing was the intensity with which I hated myself. I didn't want to feel down, but nothing worked to lighten my mood and I could barely function, so playing video games, going out, watching a movie or hanging out with friends was simply not possible. Even with as much as I loved working out, I doubt I would've been able to get to the gym, given that I had spent the past two weeks in my room and basement, coming out only a few times.

When the third week came, my depression had grown darker and I was unable to answer phone calls, shower or even eat. My mother and sister did their best to act like nothing was wrong and smile when around me, but I could see through their facades. My dad just looked worried. In many ways, my bipolar stayed hidden for as long as it did because I never let anyone, but my family see my downs. It wasn't that I knew that I was depressed and was trying to hide it, I simply didn't want to see anyone. Of course, when looking back, my family feels foolish that they didn't get me help sooner, but the truth is that bipolar disorder stays fairly hidden until it begins to rip your life apart. I just feel lucky that they loved me and did take actions once things grew worse.

I slept the days away and stayed in my dark basement bedroom. I wanted the pain to go away, but it was out of my control. When a gentle knock sounded against my door, I rolled over and faced the wall. I didn't want to see anyone, but hadn't locked my room and wasn't about to move.

My mom's voice was soft and gentle. "Kirk, can I come in?" I didn't answer, so she slowly opened the door. She noted that I was facing the wall and shook a plastic bag that she had brought into my room. Even the sound of the bag seemed distant as my mother said, "I thought you might be hungry, so I went out and picked you up a sandwich. It's your favorite."

"Thanks," I spoke just above a whisper, a strained croak. Even the simple act of speaking was growing harder, I realized. I felt exhausted from the two previous weeks and I kept thinking I just needed some rest, but I was growing more depressed and overwhelmed with each passing day. Worse, however, were the constant thoughts of suicide that I was unable to stop from picturing or thinking about. Strangely enough, as much as I wanted to end my suffering, I simply wasn't able to shake off the suffocating blanket of anguish and was therefore unable to act on any of my darker thoughts. The depression that had ensnared me felt like it was getting tighter, slowly squeezing the life out of me and I just assumed that I was going to die and that the world would be better off without me.

She set the Subway sandwich down on my dresser and came to my side. She leaned over to give me a hug in an attempt to comfort me. Instead of accepting this brave act of kindness and love, I tensed up and pushed her away, hating myself for it all the while. I wanted her to hug me, but I didn't know it and my mind was lost enough that the only thing working were my instincts. My mom's attempt was what I wanted, even if I didn't know it. I now realized that it was the physical touch that was overwhelming. I know that I would have enjoyed having someone just sit on the floor without speaking or talking to me, but even if I had been aware of what might have helped, I couldn't recognize or verbalize it.

My mother was crushed. She left the food on my dresser and quietly shut the door. With the ability to see only my own twisted reality, I was always unaware of the people around me, and especially the effects my actions had on them. In short, I was a selfish and cruel person. As my depression grew more severe over the next few days I had a hard time processing anything, especially my emotions. Nine years later, I finally understand what I was going through or what might have helped lessen my suffering. I was never a very affectionate child and now know how hard it was on my family. I can only guess how many relationships ended because I was unable to show affection.

I never ate the sub, however, as I fell into a deep sleep. I'd hit the second stage of my depression quickly and was beginning to move onto the third and final stage. My last thought before falling asleep was wishing death would take me because I was unable to take my own life.

That weekend I couldn't eat or move from my bed other than to go to the bathroom. I hadn't shaved or showered in a week and had lost enough weight to look sickly. Although my parents and sister tried to get me moving, I wasn't able to function. I wanted to die, but the effort of committing suicide was more than I could take. In many ways, I feel lucky that my deepest depressions were so extreme that they kept me from functioning for it saved my life countless times.

The next time I woke up was because my room's lights had been flicked on, the harsh light an attack on my senses. My vision was blurry and I felt confused. Although I couldn't rate how bad I had felt before falling asleep, I knew, without a doubt, that I was far worse than before. Even talking seemed like an impossible feat. Walking to the side of my bed, my sister gently touched my forearm and spoke firmly. "It's Monday and you've been sleeping for nearly two days." My sister was tired of my behavior and pulled back my sheets before continuing her motherly speech. "Your student will be here in thirty minutes, so get up and clean up now."

I tried to respond, but my voice never came. I was trying to respond, but I couldn't move, talk or think, so I simply lay there, staring up at my sister who had always tried her best to look after and protect me. Only now do I understand how lucky I was to have Chandi in my life and how hard I was on her. I couldn't take seeing the frustration bloom on my sister's face, so I closed my eyes again. Everything about my reality was overwhelming, making me feel out of place and lost, as if I didn't belong on earth or was just a dream.

"You haven't eaten in three days and you smell," Chandi said. She took hold of my arm and tried to get me moving. "Kirk," she shouted when she was unable to move me. I wasn't fighting her; I just wasn't moving, and I was far too large for Chandi's small stature to move. "You need to get up and get cleaned up or you're going to have to cancel your students." After one last tug on my arm, my sister finally gave up, dropping my arm that fell limply back to the bed. Even when I saw my sister's eyes tearing up as she stared at me, unsure of what she should do, I still didn't realize that I was causing her pain. "So you're going to cancel your students again?"

Just like my other jobs, I was an amazing worker in my beginning stages of my mania, but in the last year as my swings grew more severe, I was incapable of functioning on a steady basis. I had canceled my students two months ago and had lost two students due to my inconsistencies and it looked like the pattern was about to repeat itself.

She sensed that I wasn't going to move nor use the phone to call anyone. Chandi sighed and shook her head as she met my eyes. "Do you want me to call and cancel your students? You might lose another student." My sister waited for me to respond, but I just stared at her, with tears rolling down her cheeks. She turned and walked out my room, turning the light off before closing the door behind her. I couldn't hear her softly sobbing, but I can certainly picture it now.

Alone again, I tried to speak, but even opening my mouth felt like an overwhelming feat of strength. I didn't want to feel the way I did, but I certainly didn't know how to escape my own tortured mind. Every desire that used to drive me forward felt lost and detached from my reality. It felt like my life was a bad dream filled with false hopes and dreams. My mind was no longer functioning as I laid there trying to breathe. Suicide was now far too complicated for my fuddled thoughts to handle. If I couldn't speak, shower, shave, eat or move, I certainly wasn't able to take my own life. Therefore, I closed my eyes again, screaming inside but unable to voice my pain. My body didn't seem like it belonged to me and I felt empty, wondering why the world even wanted me to wake up yet again.

For two more weeks I was unable to break through the cage of depression that continued to tighten around me. I had been bad before, but this was the first time I hadn't been able to move or talk. After three days of my worst depression my mother had come into my room. Even without the light turned on it was easy to see that her face was somber as she sat down beside me.

"Kirk, I think you need help." Had I cared about anything or been able to think, I'm sure I would have denied my mom's hypothesis, but I was lost in the overwhelming pain I felt. I just wanted the suffering to stop. "I called the doctor and he gave me the name of a good psychiatrist. The soonest I could get us in to see him was in two weeks. I can't do this anymore."

With that statement, my mother stood up and left the room. Even then, unable to eat, move or care about anything, I didn't realize anything was wrong. I was sure that it was the world that was twisted and not my mind. I was wrong.

PART TWO: NOWHERE LEFT TO RUN

:: Seeking Help Even When The Truth Hurts :

I. SEEKING HELP

It doesn't take long when looking back at my life and my behavior to realize how lucky I am to be alive. I wouldn't be had my family not known that I was beyond helping myself. Although I had seen psychologists in my youth, it was because I was difficult, and my mom was trying her best to understand and help me. When my mother made an appointment with one of the leading psychiatrists in Colorado, I was very aware of the difference. I wasn't seeing a psychiatrist because I was in need of some simple guidance. This time, I was seeing a specialist because my family had run out of options and believed something was truly wrong with me.

I admit without a doubt in my mind I was desperately in need of help, but at the time I felt betrayed by those who were supposed to love me the most. Believing fully that I was just having a rough time, I truly couldn't see or understand just how serious of a risk I was to myself and others. Even had the bipolar not blurred my vision to reality, no one wants to believe there is something wrong with them and I was no exception. I didn't like seeing a doctor for a cough, but I despised the idea of seeing a specialist when the sole purpose was to determine my sanity. Although I didn't want to waste my time seeing another therapist I was still trapped in my depression and I didn't have the energy to fight or run. That double-edged sword had struck again. When the time came I reluctantly got into the car with my mom as we drove off to meet a top psychiatrist that I will refer to as Dr. Smith. Although the worst of my depression had faded, I was still irritable and moving or leaving was quite difficult for me.

During the drive I sat quietly in the car, staring out the window as we drove by a rundown amusement park that was on the way to Dr. Smith's office. When the tall buildings started rising into the sky around us I knew we were getting close. Not only did I not want to speak to anyone, I certainly didn't feel like speaking to a stranger. What is still strange to me is that I didn't feel any apprehension. I truly believed that there was nothing wrong with me. It had been a hard few weeks and I felt like my family was exaggerating every time I spoke. I was actually expecting to hear the psychiatrist tell my mother that she was simply worrying for nothing, but I didn't have the energy to fight with my mother about the merits of seeing the psychiatrist.

The large parking lot was shaded by the immense gray stone building. My mom parked, turned off the radio and turned to face me. "Thank you for trying this, honey." My mother looked over at me with her warm blue eyes filled with worry.

I sighed and nodded as I opened the door. I never realized that when I was down I walked hunched over, my head down and focused on the ground, but I did. Not only did my posture change depending on my moods, analyzing old pictures shows that my eyes were dull and empty when I was down and brilliant and wild when manic. It is amazing and sad how unaware of my behavior I truly was. Seeing only my own reality had cost me everything, but I wouldn't realize that until years later.

I stared at the dirty, oil-stained pavement, then followed my mom as if there were an invisible chain connected to her. Convinced I was fine, I didn't want to waste my time or my parents' money to hear what I already knew. Had I more energy, I would've fought seeing a specialist with every ounce of my strength, but I had only just begun to come out of my depression.

The two glass doors that stood at the entrance to the building were heavy as we walked into a large marble entryway. Severe, imposing, and empty. To my left there was a bank and to my right two elevators I wasn't looking forward to entering.

I knew that it I had more energy I wouldn't have gotten onto the elevator. Diagnosing bipolar is very difficult for a variety of reasons, and one of them is many people go to the psychiatrist alone. Then, depending on their mood, they are either doing great or life is horrible. To properly diagnose bipolar, I now realize how important it is to have someone close to the individual to fill in the blanks for the psychiatrist.

"Come on," my mother took hold of my arm with a gentle grip, guiding me onto the elevator. I noted another woman on the elevator who looked at me with what felt like caution. I'm not a big man, so I didn't understand why the woman with her straight brown hair and hazel eyes was staring at me. I hated when people stared at me, judging me, so I stared back, waiting for her to look away. As if sensing the tension, my mother pulled me to the back of the elevator, pressing a button while making small talk with the woman that had quickly looked away from me. Oftentimes I would feel like people were staring at me, judging me, and at my manic peaks, plotting against me.

What makes these times so hypocritical is how I always judged others without a second glance. Looking back, it is appalling to realize how quickly I decided if someone was a friend or foe. Like my emotions, there were only extremes and no room for middle ground. Good friendships and relationships were ruined because of the tricks my mind and moods played on me. When I was manic or depressed my view of life and everything in it was twisted, always leading me to act out in ways that were far beyond reason.

In the rare moments when I was between mania and depression I did have a good sense of people; however those moments were both rare and fleeting. This made relationships, both personal and professional nearly impossible to nurture. Relationships are hard enough when thinking clearly and calmly, but the reality I observed through my bipolar eyes was never calm and often warped. Because of this, I pushed people away and always ended up alone.

My warped worldview affected my life in many ways other than just my relationships. In fact, many of my major life decisions were made after paranoia, anger, mistrust and delusions led me to form false conclusions. What baffles me is how dedicated I was to my worldview. If I decided I wouldn't like something, I hated it and there was not a force strong enough to change my mind. The same was true with what I liked, or rather what I knew instantly beyond a doubt what I would like, before trying it out.

When I was lost in the depths of a manic or depressive swing, the decisions I made, logical or not, were carved in stone. I would make rash decisions or come to a radical conclusion that others saw as comical, strange or horrific. No matter how large or drastic my decisions were, once my mind was made up, I was committed deeply and never thought twice about my resulting actions. This went for people, art, clothing, food, school work, music, and pretty much everything in life.

As usual I had already made up my mind about the woman that had briefly met my eyes. I didn't like her. Instead of looking at her, I stared into the mirrors that lined the elevator and rested on a polished marble base.

And though it was a beautiful elevator, all I could focus on were the fingerprints and smears on the polished surfaces.

When the elevator began to move, I continued to stick to the idea that seeing a shrink was a waste of time. Not only was it in the middle of the day, but it was different. I had always been very methodical and I hated change, something I have found to be very common in others suffering from bipolar. I wasn't scared, but I wasn't happy. When the door opened and the woman stepped off, I said in a loud voice, "Have a nice day, ma'am." My words were harsh and filled with sarcasm.

Whether I was manic or lightly depressed I was often very aggressive. In the beginning stages of my manic episodes my aggression would manifest itself in different ways. Sometimes it would make me more brazen when approaching a woman or more playful with jokes. In the later stages of my manic episodes, I would become easily agitated, often leading me to start fights with people who weren't even looking at me. During my depressions I was often irritable, impatient and mean.

Clearly, the woman had done nothing wrong, but she quickened her pace as if threatened. I felt satisfaction until I noticed my mother's stare. "What? She was giving me a nasty look for no reason?"

"I thought you promised me you would give this a try?" My mother's tone was serious as she stared me down. "You gave me your word."

Although there was not much that remained steady in my life, I did have a strong sense of honor and when I gave my word, I would try my best to keep it. The only times I ever broke my word was when I was at the peak stage of either depression or mania. Of course, I was never aware that I had broken my word, but now, as I analyze my past with a clear and balanced mind, I see how fickle even my honor was. "Fine," I said, pulling myself away and crossing my arms defiantly. I would keep my word. "Sorry," I added without any sincerity.

The elevator stopped and made an annoying dinging sound as the doors slid open. "Here we are," my mother said, offering a gentle smile as she stepped off and walked to the wall directly across from the elevators. I reluctantly followed, staring at the list of names and office numbers my mother was checking. "This won't take long. Just remember that you promised me you would cooperate."

I huffed and I followed her, my favorite yellow jacket was too warm for the weather, but I didn't really notice. My mind was focused on the doors as we passed by. I didn't feel any anxiousness as the office numbers grew closer to our destination, but I didn't want to be there. Had I been manic there was no way I would've agreed to see a psychiatrist. Luckily I felt like walking was difficult. I certainly didn't have enough energy to resist, so I followed behind my mother, my eyes always returning to my feet as we neared Dr. Smith's office.

Dr. Smith, a highly regarded psychiatrist, had been suggested to us by multiple doctors, but I wasn't sold. I don't think there were enough credentials in the world to convince me that I wasn't wasting my time. When my mom came to the door at the end of the hallway and opened it, I paused for a split second before entering the waiting room.

I headed over to the couches that encircled a nice table filled with magazines, then plopped down and grabbed a random magazine while my mom checked me in and filled out the paperwork. It's sad for me to think that my mom even had to fill out my papers, but I was never cooperative when it came to something I didn't agree with.

After my mom finished with the paperwork and handed it to the nurse. I felt she seemed extremely grumpy. She pressed a small red button on the wall before speaking, "Mrs. Miller, Dr. Smith will be right with you. Just sit down and make yourself comfortable."

When the door opened, a man stepped forward. I couldn't help but appraise him. He was dressed in a maroon sweater, nice slacks and polished wing-tip shoes that looked expensive. He glanced briefly at the receptionist and then locked his psychiatric gaze on me. He was bald except for the slightly curly gray hair sticking out beyond his ears and resting low on his hawk nose was a pair of thin, rectangular glasses. He looked like they had pulled a psychiatrist out of the movies to play his part. He met my eyes over the edges of those glasses. "Kirk, I presume?" Although he spoke quietly, his voice felt cold to me. In retrospect, I'm sure he was a really good guy, especially when having to deal with individuals like me on a daily basis.

I nodded and stood up slowly, not looking forward to the next hour and a half. My mom stood up with more speed, moving around the waiting room table and extending her hand as she introduced herself. "Dr. Smith, I'm Jeanne Miller. We spoke on the phone." She gestured to me, she added, "and this is my son, Kirk." I reached out and shook the man's hand out of courtesy as my mom added, "Thank you so much for fitting us in."

"It is nice to meet you both," Dr. Smith responded. He opened the thick wooden door of the waiting room with one hand and gestured down the hallway with his other. "If you would follow me, my office is at the end of the hall." The way Dr. Smith spoke was very calculated, as was his gaze. Even when shaking hands, I had the feeling he was analyzing everything about me. Of course I was looking for excuses to dislike the entire experience.

He led us down the hallway and opened the door to his corner office. He gestured towards the leather chairs and sofas, and spoke with his characteristic, gentle and measured tone. "Please, sit down."

The view was beautiful, overlooking a lake framed by some of Colorado's signature mountains. I sat down in the soft leather couch across from his desk and tried to make myself comfortable. My mother sat next to me. Dr. Smith pulled out a yellow legal pad and pen along with a file that must have come from the other doctors and psychologists I had seen over the years. I had been officially diagnosed with ADHD and had seen at least three psychologists, taking a very expensive test for one of them that I assumed was included in the file that Dr. Smith opened up. Unlike when I went to see a psychologist, this wasn't to work on family or school problems. This time, I was very aware that it was my sanity that was being evaluated. I didn't feel fear, for I knew I was fine. I had no idea that my entire life was about to change.

II. DIAGNOSIS AND DISBLIEF

Due to the difficulty of diagnosing bipolar properly, psychiatrists have grown very cautious before labeling someone with such a serious diagnosis. The first thing the psychiatrist has to be sure of is that their patient's behavior is not the direct result of any medical issues, medications or illicit drugs that could cause some of the same symptoms found in bipolar. After they are sure that the behavior is the result of a true condition, they have to rule out a long list of other mental disorders that can have very similar symptoms to bipolar. Luckily, our family doctor had made sure that the psychiatrist had all the information he needed.

Even before I went to see Dr. Smith, I had endured countless blood tests to ensure that my behavior was not the result of an undiscovered medical condition and I had also seen a few psychologists who had given me standard tests like the MMPI-2 (Minnesota Multiphasic Personality Inventory) as well as adding their personal opinions.

After my mother and I sat down on the soft leather couch, Dr. Smith joined us, sitting down in an expensive, plush chair rather than his antique wooden desk, directly across from the couch. Dr. Smith seemed to have forgotten the thick manila folder that contained my medical history, and leaned backward before reaching out to grab it from his desk. I stared at the folder.. My medical tests had all come back normal, so I already knew that I was healthy. All I had to do was put up with one more doctor and his questions to prove once and for all that I was fine.

Dr. Smith crossed his legs, carefully scanning the file that he was obviously already familiar with. For a few minutes, we sat in silence as Dr. Smith proved that he was just as meticulous and cautious as we had been told. To me, he felt cold and calculating, but I wasn't happy about anything that morning.

Finally, Dr. Smith appeared ready, because he met my gaze. "Do you mind if I ask you some questions?"

I remember sighing. I had been through this before and wasn't looking forward to answering the same questions that all the other mental professionals had asked. To my surprise, his questions were very different than what I was expecting. Most of the questions were very simple, needing little time to give my cold response. After about ten minutes, Dr. Smith paused, lifting his long legal pad and his pen to make a few notes. When the questions continued, they became more obscure, some that were easy to answer and others that I had to stop and contemplate before answering. He'd pause occasionally before asking another question, I found myself growing curious about what he was writing about me. Suddenly, however, his questions became very detailed. Due to my curiosity, I had let down my guard and found myself answering truthfully. The odd part was that sometimes my responses surprised me. It was clear that Dr. Smith was not like the other doctors and psychologists I had seen. As the questions became very personal, I hesitated. I had promised to cooperate, but I was very aware that my mother was there. As if she sensed my worry, she simply patted me on the leg as if trying to comfort me. I answered all the questions as best I could, attempting to gauge Dr. Smith's reaction to my responses.

Unfortunately, his face never gave anything away. I was good at reading people, so I didn't like the fact that I couldn't glean any information from Dr. Smith.

Dr. Smith paused and turned his calculating eyes to his notes before turning to my mother. When he asked my mother about some of my responses, I was astonished and angry as I listened to her disagree with me. Not only did my mother contradict some of my answers but she went into detail about my behavior. I was shocked to hear how my explosive and violent responses affected my family. I knew my mother well enough to tell that she was trying her best to hold back tears as she spoke of my outbursts and how they had continued to worsen throughout the years.

Perhaps she mentioned the mailbox incident because she felt as if we had moved beyond the scope of our family. Essentially, I took out all my anger on the mailbox that was at the edge of the property. She could tolerate broken doors inside our home, but temper and destruction in front of our entire neighborhood was something that had impacted her. Holes in the walls, planning down a wooden door at 1 am because it stuck a little bit also seemed to have upset her.

To me, the stories my mother was telling felt exaggerated and false. I felt betrayed and angry, but I also knew that my mother was trying to help me, or at least she believed her accounts of my life and actions were accurate. She truly believed what she was saying, leaving me feeling a bit confused and entrapped.

Why is she lying? I wondered. I sat in stunned silence, fists tightly clenched, listening as she told story after story of when my outbursts caused trouble for me, my sister and my parents. She even told stories of me as a child, when I tried to jump out of our car while we were driving on I-70. I remembered the stories, but they felt distant and false the way she described them. Surely I wasn't as dangerous or unhinged as she made me seem.

Tired of listening, I interrupted. "This is ridiculous." Something in my voice surprised me: doubt. It was as if I wasn't sure which, her stories or my memories were real.

Dr. Smith leaned back in his seat, taking his glasses off and holding them in his right hand as he looked between me and his notes. He let the silence stretch out for a time, then took a deep breath before putting his glasses back on. Dr. Smith ignored my interruption and returned to asking me questions. Now that I was certain I was under attack, I listened to every question carefully before answering. I wasn't going to be caught off guard again. After a bit more than an hour, Dr. Smith finally put down his pen.

Again he removed his glasses, met my eyes, and set his hands down in his lap before leaning forward. "Kirk, you certainly have ADHD as Dr. Hudson diagnosed in your teens, but there are far more serious problems that we need to address." Dr. Smith picked up my medical file once again, referring to the notes of the other psychologist who had worked with me before continuing. "From everything in your file, your tests, behavior, the notes of the other psychologists and from everything I have heard today, I have no doubt that you have an extremely severe case of Bipolar I. Although you do exhibit some psychotic symptoms, that is not uncommon with bipolar." I was about to speak but realized that he wasn't done. "You also have generalized and social anxiety."

"What?" I said, not sure exactly how offended I should be. I didn't feel fear, especially when it came to other people, so how could I have anxiety?

"What exactly does all that mean?" my mother asked. She took my hand as she waited to hear the news. I had always been fascinated with mental disorders and had taken a few psychology classes that had briefly gone over bipolar among other mental disorders, so I knew the answer before Dr. Smith began.

"Bipolar has no cure and it has been shown to get worse with time." My mother was trying her best to hold herself together, but I could tell she was in pain. "The good news is that we have medications that will help your son manage his condition." Dr. Smith paused and I could sense that he really didn't want to continue talking, but he continued. "It is my job to be honest so that you, your son and family go into his treatment with realistic expectations."

My mother was nervous and held her hands together as she spoke, "I understand. Please continue."

"With such a severe case, even with medication, it is important to realize that there is a strong possibility that he will never lead a normal life." Dr. Smith turned to me as he continued. "I would highly suggest that you also continue to see someone. If you would like to work with someone other than me, I would understand and can give you some names. Bipolar I is a serious disorder and should not be taken lightly. Your son needs treatment, both with medications and weekly sessions if he hopes to have a chance at holding a job or relationship."

I was about to request other names as I stared angrily at Dr. Smith, but my mother spoke first. "I would prefer that we continue to see you. Every doctor we spoke to suggested that we see you, so do you have the time?" I could tell that my mother was clinging to the hope that Dr. Smith would say yes, but as he nodded, she took a deep breath and asked: "I know this is not a polite question, but I must ask. Is there any way that your diagnosis is wrong?"

"Mrs. Miller, you must understand that I do not come to such a devastating diagnosis lightly." Dr. Smith rested his hand on the manila folder in his lap as if for confirmation, and his voice was gentle in addressing my mother. "I reviewed your son's file multiple times before today, looking carefully through the many notes from his doctors and psychologists for anything that might point to something other than bipolar. Unfortunately, everyone your son has seen is highly respected and also believed Kirk was bipolar. Between the results of his psychological tests, the previous psychologists' notes and everything I have heard today, I am quite comfortable with my assessment and it is my professional opinion that your son needs help."

"I think we should get a second opinion," I said. The anger and frustration built with each word.

Dr. Smith met my accusatory stare. "Kirk, you have every right to seek a second opinion and I will even give you names, but I must be honest with you. In my opinion, every psychiatrist that reviews this file and speaks with you and your family will come to the same conclusion. I apologize for breaking such news to you, but this is a serious disorder. Personally, I feel it would be best if you began taking medication immediately. I would also like to see you next week if that is possible."

My mother did her best to hold back her tears, but a few slid down her cheeks. As for me, I simply stared at Dr. Smith. I hated him and everything about the diagnoses. I didn't have bipolar and I didn't need medication. Unfortunately, I knew that what I thought was no longer part of the equation. The expert had spoken, and I knew my mother would listen.

Since I was living at home with no job and tuition bills I had two choices, I could run away or try the medications and the therapy. I wanted to run, but watching my mother write a check she couldn't afford to the psychiatrist, I figured I'd play along. In all honesty, I just didn't have the drive to run away. Had I been manic, I know I would've stormed out of the psychiatrist's office long before he was able to write a fist-full of prescriptions and blood test orders. I wasn't manic, however, so I sighed and let my head fall back against the couch. The double-edged sword had cut both ways again. Between hearing that there was no cure and I would never be free of medication, I remember clearly wondering if my family would be better off if I was gone.

III. GIVING IN TO MEDICATION

The trip home was long; my mother tried to talk about anything but the heavy truth hanging over us both. I was just looking forward to getting home and taking a long nap where my sleep would take me away from reality. I didn't know much about Lithium or the other drugs Dr. Smith had written prescriptions for, but I wondered what they did and how they would affect me. I had tried enough drugs that I was slightly curious, but every time I tried to relax, my mind returned to the same moment in the psychiatrist's office. Dr. Smith had been very clear that there was no cure, although we might be able to manage the symptoms and keep my outbursts to a minimum. I didn't care about managing my symptoms, for all I kept hearing was that there was no cure. Knowing I was going to be on medication for the rest of my life without even a guarantee that I would get better was hard to swallow.

On our way home, my mother stopped by the Walgreens near our house, handing the pharmacist the fist-full of prescriptions that needed to be filled, along with her credit card. My mother had tried to hide how much the single visit to Dr. Smith had cost, but I had caught a glimpse of the check when she handed it over. Six hundred dollars was far more than my mother or father could afford and I knew that monthly bills for medication would only add strain to my mother. I didn't feel bad, but I felt angry that my mother had been fooled by a smooth-talking shrink, although years later I would realize just how correct Dr. Smith had been.

The only reason I would take the medication was because I had given my mother my word. When we returned home, I was heading towards the basement door when my mother called out. "Dr. Smith said you should start your medications today."

I sighed and turned back around, then headed into the kitchen. My mom carefully read the labels before handing me three pills from the Lithium bottle and a tiny round pill from the bottle labeled Klonopin. I didn't hesitate, but instead tossed the pills into my mouth and stuck my head under the sink. Whatever the pills were, I was confident they wouldn't be nearly as potent as some of the drugs I had taken in the past. I was very wrong. The drugs they gave me to control my swings were stronger than most drugs I could get on the street, only these had no positive effects.

After swallowing the pills, I turned away from the sink as my mother walked up to me. Her face was drawn and sad as she wrapped her thin arms around my waist. It was clear that Dr. Smith's explanation of what bipolar was had left my mother worried. I had stopped listening when he had explained that I was currently recovering from 'a major depressive episode' and that it would take time for the medications to work. What I gathered was that Dr. Smith thought I needed to be carefully monitored. "Are you okay?" My mother asked gently as I pulled away.

"I'm tired," I answered truthfully, before turning and vanishing into the basement.

My basement bedroom remained blessedly dark throughout the day, and I collapsed on my bed. The day felt oddly distant and dreamlike. Only now do I realize how odd it was that, on the very day I was diagnosed with a major mental illness, I didn't wonder or worry about my mind or the medications I would be taking for the rest of my life. Had I felt better, I might have smiled at how absurd the psychiatrist had been, but I wasn't ready to smile yet.

The clock next to my bed informed me it was a bit past four in the afternoon. I sighed. All I wanted was to escape the world. I figured I'd watch some television before heading to bed, then wondered when I would start feeling energetic again. I know now that what I was craving was to feel manic again, but I simply thought I was tired. Even before the medications had a chance to begin to work, my depression continued to fade. For the first day in weeks I didn't think of suicide, but I had just taken the pills and knew they wouldn't work that fast. The psychiatrist had been right that I was recovering from a deep depression, but I didn't know it at the time and certainly couldn't see it. My so-called 'swings' were as natural to me as breathing, making it impossible to look inward and see the truth of my situation. Only now can I look back and objectively analyze what I was going through. After watching some television, I returned to my room and collapsed on my bed. When I closed my eyes, sleep came hard and fast.

The next morning, I awoke to a gentle knock at my door. "Kirk, can mom and I come in?" my sister asked.

I was surprised that I was still tired; the clock read nine in the morning. "Come on in," I answered slowly as I rubbed my eyes. I didn't feel any different from taking the doctor's medication, but I hadn't expected to. There was a sense of slight satisfaction that the medication hadn't done anything, but that vanished as my mother and sister came in with concern on their faces. "What's wrong?"

My sister came over and gave me a big hug. "Mom and dad told me everything. How are you holding up?"

I shook her off, annoyed at being reminded of the previous day. Until my sister had brought it up, the previous day's events were absent from my thoughts. "I'm fine."

My mom extended her hand and I stared at it. Oh. Pills. "Your father said that you could take your pills in the morning or at night." My dad was a great pharmacist and would have made an amazing doctor. I didn't listen to many people, but when it came to medicine, I listened when my dad gave advice. "I also wanted to remind you that next week we have an appointment with Dr. Smith again. Your father would like to come as well, if that's okay?"

It was clear that everyone was worried, and I wasn't in the mood to deal with anyone. I snatched them and threw them into my mouth, reached for my bottle of water that I kept next to my bed, and swallowed the pills before lashing out. "I'll take the damn pills in the morning, but I could use a day without being interrogated." My family, friends and loved ones never deserved to be spoken to the way I often did. They cared for me and often took the brunt of my frustration, anger or sadness at the world I saw. Although I'm a completely different person now, it pains me to look at how I treated those that cared for me and see the trauma I caused everyone who grew close to me. "I hope what happened yesterday will remain within the family." I wasn't crazy and certainly didn't want any women I dated or my friends to think otherwise. It was the first time I felt the stigma that was forever intertwined with my life.

"Of course we won't tell anyone," my mother and sister said at nearly the same time.

"Just leave me alone, okay?" My voice was hollow and cold.

Instead of asking why I wanted to be alone or trying to make me feel better, my mother and sister just nodded and left the room. The fact that my mother and sister did not like leaving things unresolved only made the ease of getting them to leave feel odd. My sister was always trying to lift my spirits or calm me down in an effort to keep the family from fighting. It was a burden she should not have tried to shoulder, but I'm not sure our family would have survived without her. My father was always the calm one in our family, but my mother fed off of my energy, making every swing I went through affect the entire family. Many times, my explosions caused fights between my mother and father, again leaving my sister struggling to calm everyone down. I do admit that our family put on a good show. To everyone who didn't live with us, we looked like a normal family. The truth, however, was that I was putting a strain on everyone close to me and we were far from normal. Our family was suffering, and I have no illusions that I was responsible for a large part of it.

After my door closed, I heard my mother and sister begin to cry. I didn't feel guilt, but annoyance. I covered my ears with my pillows. I was agitated but I didn't feel any more energetic than the previous day. My stomach rumbled when I rolled over. It had been awhile since I had eaten and I was hungry, but I still wasn't ready to leave my room. Well aware that my sister and mother had probably spent hours researching bipolar, I wasn't in the mood to talk about my supposed insanity. Many might claim that I was in denial, but the terrifying part of bipolar is that even at the peaks of my mania or depression, I couldn't see the reality of my actions or life. Even with the medications, I never felt like there was anything wrong with me.

I closed my eyes and silently begged for sleep. For the next few days, I came out of my room only for food and to take the medications that were supposed to help me to be 'normal'. It was always hard to tell how long I would stay in the late stage of my depression, but after a few days I began to feel a bit better. I certainly wasn't feeling great, but I shaved, showered and ate. My depression was fading, but following closely behind was another round of mania. It was always just a matter of time.

Looking back, perhaps the clearest sign that my depression was fading was that colors seemed brighter, unlike the darker shades of gray I would see when I was in the final stage of my depression. My favorite color growing up was always black, not because I liked black, but because I truly didn't like any color. With the aid of hindsight, my darkest depressions always seemed to dim the world around me into pale shades. It was usually the first sign that I was heading to a deeper depression.

After the diagnosis, nothing really changed. My family continued to walk on eggshells around me, although I didn't realize it. Eventually I wondered if the medication was actually working, and I spoke with my dad. When it came to medications, he was a great pharmacist and had a knack of explaining medications in a way that always answered my questions. That morning, my dad and I were sitting alone, giving me the opportunity to ask him some questions while my sister and mother were away. "So, what is Lithium?"

"It is a medication prescribed in order to stabilize your moods. It's even called a mood-stabilizer," my dad answered gently.

"So how does it work?"

"No one really knows," my dad answered honestly. He stood up from the kitchen table and looked at my prescription, as if holding the bottle would give him some insight. "You're just starting, so it will take a few weeks to get your blood level stabilized."

"So that's why I have to take a blood test every week?" My father nodded and walked back to the table.

"Correct. They have to be careful with such a potent medication, so Dr. Smith is doing a good job. Just so you know, it may take a while to level out your blood level. Usually it's used along with other medication, but Dr. Smith may want to get your Lithium level stable before adding anything, which is common practice."

I couldn't get past what he had said earlier in the conversation. "They really don't know how it works?"

My father nodded. "Many of the drugs they use to treat bipolar are new drugs and because we don't know what causes bipolar, we really don't know how many of the bipolar medications work, but that doesn't change the fact that they have been shown to help. They do work, so you need to listen to Dr. Smith and take your meds. Just because no one really understands how the drugs work doesn't mean that they haven't been shown to be effective."

"So," I hesitated, then decided to finish my question. "Do you think I'm bipolar?"

My dad paused, scratching his thick brown beard before sighing. "I'm afraid if I look at your behavior as objectively as I can..." my father paused, his bushy eyebrows lowering over his eyes as he looked down.

"Even you think I'm nuts?" I was eating cereal at the time, and now instead of a meal it became a convenient weapon to show my father what I thought about his guilty verdict. Walking over the sink, I dropped my bowl of cereal in, ignoring the noise it made and not caring whether or not it broke.

"I don't, but perhaps the medications will help," my father said gently, always the optimist.

Over the next month, multiple blood tests, and seeing Dr. Smith twice more, my Lithium dosage was increased dramatically, and I was prescribed three more medications to help keep my bipolar in check. To say that the medications did affect me is a gross understatement, only they didn't stop the swings. The medications may have helped slow how often I had a manic or depressive episode, but each mania or depression continued to grow more severe, no matter how much Dr. Smith increased the number or dosage of my medications.

Important note: To everyone reading this memoir, I must make one thing very clear. Had I not sought medical help and taken my prescribed medication, I would not be around now to tell my story. As I talk about what happened to me and the side effects I encountered when taking bipolar medications, it is important for everyone dealing with bipolar to fully understand that I strongly support the brilliant researchers and doctors that are currently working on treating bipolar and DO NOT condone or advocate any action without the formal advice and guidance of a trained medical professional.

IV. TRYING TO FIND STABILITY

After a few months of constant blood tests and some setbacks leading to an increase in my medications, I was growing tired of being poked and prodded. Feeling like a lab rat was not working for me and it felt like my life revolved around medical appointments and sessions with Dr. Smith. With nearly every blood test I took or session with Dr. Smith, a new medication would be added, or my dosage adjusted. Many times, a new drug would be added to counteract the side effects of my current medications. The entire process was tiring and the only reason that I continued to go was because I had promised my mother. In all respects, even with the medications and sessions with Dr. Smith, I wasn't improving.

One of the biggest problems with the frequency of all my appointments and medical tests was that it was beginning to cause tension between me and Vanya, as I will refer to her. Vanya was my girlfriend then and we were becoming more seriously involved, but I wasn't about to tell her about my bipolar. Even if I still felt that nothing was wrong with me, I didn't want others judging me.

As a soft-spoken Polish girl with striking blue eyes and a kind heart, I knew that Vanya would not understand. Besides, I didn't feel like I was keeping anything from her as I was still unable to see the reality of my life. As we became more serious, I asked her to move in with me. Like always, I was taking actions based on the present, unaware of the complications that living with someone might entail. Since she was already a student at a nearby college, she agreed and we moved in together.

When she moved in with me, however, it became harder to hide what I was going through. Not only did I have to schedule all my medical appointments when she had class and take my medication when she wasn't paying attention, I was actually annoyed with her for inconveniencing me, unaware that I was the one hiding a serious truth from her. As usual, I was unable to see her point of view, thinking only of myself I never thought of taking her feelings into account.

After being diagnosed, I was curious to see how other people viewed bipolar. What I found was that the disorder was widely misunderstood and, in many cases, viewed as a mild inconvenience. As I spoke to people, asking their opinion of bipolar, there were two very distinctive groups. The first group viewed bipolar as an excuse for an individual to act out while avoiding responsibility. These individuals had no sympathy for anyone with bipolar, but not because they were bad people. They simply hadn't dealt with someone with bipolar and had no experience with the devastation the disorder could cause. I couldn't fault them for their lack of understanding as I was just beginning to research bipolar myself. Although I didn't believe I had bipolar, I was still curious to learn about it. My understanding of what bipolar was came slowly as the only time I was able to research was during the first stage of my mania. The search went slowly, but the information began to trickle in.

The second group had the opposite view because they had directly seen or been involved with someone with bipolar. These people tightened up even thinking about their experiences and were extremely cautious with their words and opinions. More than once, my gentle questions brought tears to the person's face and many couldn't even talk about their experiences dealing with a loved one who suffered with it. Having seen the true destructive power of bipolar, these individuals spoke about it as if it was a life-threatening disease. To be fair, I agree more with the second group as many that I spoke to had lost a family member in some tragic way. Each one of these individuals wanted to stay as far away from bipolar as they could, some of them telling horrific stories where they had felt threatened and endangered just being around their sibling, partner or spouse. With such extreme views, neither group made me feel like making my diagnosis public would be a good idea. Therefore, I decided to keep my diagnosis, as false as I felt it to be, a secret from everyone. That included my friends and, of course, Vanya.

Keeping it a secret became harder as time went on and the medications began to cause both common and more severe side effects. Not only did I begin to suffer from more common side effects, but I discovered not listed, including a complete loss of interest in things like playing the violin or painting. As these began to become severe enough that the people closest to me began to notice, I became quite adept at lying about why I was losing my hair or was having a hard time retaining my short-term memory.

When the doctor increased my Lithium dosage to 1800 milligrams daily, my blood test showed that I was extremely close to a toxic level. Like many people taking large doses of lithium, my thyroid burned out and yet another medication was added to a growing list that I was incapable of following. Had my mother not set out my pills, I wouldn't have been able to keep up with all the daily medications I had to take.

As my hair continued to thin I began to have problems with simple motor skills. My hands would shake so badly that often food would fall from my fork before reaching my mouth. These side effects, along with the mental fog they caused made me want to stop taking my medications, but I kept my word to my mother and took my pills every morning. Eventually, my mind was so drugged, I would stare off into the distance, unable to think or care. As time passed, I felt that for every side effect the doctors had another medication to help, but the game of balancing my medications became quite frustrating.

Although my family and Dr. Smith felt that I was finally reaching some level of stability, I felt more drugged and sedated than ever, and that included drugs like opium, heroin, and other street drugs. In many ways, I was surprised how powerful the medications I took really were. My mind that I had always treasured felt heavy and my thoughts were slow and muddled. To be blunt, I didn't feel like myself and my life was quickly losing its clarity as I was trapped in a mental fog that took away my creativity, aspirations and passions. Luckily, even with the medications, I was still unaware of reality and didn't notice what I had lost or gained.

The worst part was that I wasn't even aware that two of my greatest passions had vanished. Unfinished paintings hung on the walls and my manuscripts were left incomplete, not that I cared. Everything in my life had become like my manuscripts and paintings, unfinished and unpolished. Although I had appeared to turn a corner, remaining 'stable' for nearly two full months, I wasn't happy, nor did I feel like myself. As my medication increased, everything that I had always loved about myself was vanishing. Nearly at the two-month mark, everyone, including me, was in for quite a surprise.

V. UNDER THE INFLUENCE

Unable to hide my growing side effects, Vanya eventually began to worry, wondering what had happened to the man that she had first fallen for. Just as everyone was beginning to think the medications were working, I fell into a depression. Although the time between my swings had been a bit slower, the medications were unable to completely stop them. The worst part was that when I did fall into my first depression since starting my treatments, it was far more severe than the previous down. Since I had seemed stable for two long months, my crash surprised everyone. Like Dr. Smith had warned on my first visit with him, even with all the medications there was no guarantee that I would, or could, lead a normal life.

As my grades continued to slip and I was lost in a deep depression, Vanya kept wondering if she had done something to upset me. Unable to communicate with any skill, Vanya packed up a travel bag and left to stay with her parents for a few weeks. Not only did I not care that she was gone, I was lucky she had left when she did as my depression quickly grew more severe. Hopelessness stole over me, and I wondered why I was even bothering to take my medications. My world lost all color, vibrancy and joy and my mind was overtaken by the worst darkness I had ever experienced. When I fell into a catatonic state, my mother contacted the doctors who prescribed yet another medication in an attempt to help me. Although I hated Dr. Smith and the other doctors that I dealt with, I know now that they were trying their best to fight a battle they had no chance of winning. When Vanya returned two weeks later, my depression had come and gone, only this time, instead of coming to a short-lived neutral state of stability, I felt my mind overtake my medications as the first stage of mania hit me hard. I was on enough drugs to knock out a horse, but when I began to swing, there was no amount of medication that could temper the ferocity of my ups or downs. In fact, as time went on, my swings continued to grow more severe. Even with great help and medication to stabilize and keep me under control, I was losing my mind, although hindsight tells me that it had always been broken.

My sudden and intense swings shocked and surprised my family, my doctor, and Vanya. I was on the maximum allowed dosage of my many medications, so Dr. Smith wasn't sure why I was still suffering from manic and depressive episodes. He tried his best to stabilize me, but there was nothing he could do. Vanya was glad to see me laughing again, but she had never experienced the later stages of my manias, setting her up for quite a rude awakening.

Once again my mania began to take over, and I decided that it was high time I started doing my own research. There had to be something that Dr. Smith could prescribe that wouldn't make my mind feel so dull. Although I had lost my passions, I became obsessed with researching bipolar, at least when I was at the beginning stage of my manias.

When Dr. Smith added Depakote, an anticonvulsant medication that had proven to be successful in helping to control bipolar symptoms, my side effects worsened but my mania continued to build up its strength. Although I continued to crack jokes, when Vanya watched my hands shake so badly that I dropped a glass of water, she demanded answers.

"Are you okay? Why do your hands always shake and how come I feel like you're hiding something from me?"

"It runs in the family," I responded without a moment's hesitation. I am not proud of it now, but lying had always been an integral part of my life. Reading people and knowing what to say, while also believing the lies I told, was an important part of my self-preservation. Whether it was dealing with a police officer or a girlfriend, lying was like second nature. The most interesting part is that I never really thought about lying, it just came. I'd lied to my live-in girlfriend like it was nothing. I was more lost than ever.

"What is going on with you?" Vanya was tearing up. "Two weeks ago you wouldn't even hug me and now you can't stop smiling. Is it something I did or are you trying to push me away?"

"What?" I snapped. Vanya's eyes widened at the sudden ferocity. As I had done all my life, when someone reached out to comfort and understand me, I grew cold and felt like I needed to distance myself. My mania was gaining momentum, so I had no ability to see Vanya's point of view. To me, she was prying, and it made me angry. I still didn't believe I had bipolar and I certainly wasn't going to go around explaining why my hands shook, especially when she couldn't take my word for it. "Why are you pushing me? I already told you, it runs in the family and is no big deal. What is your problem?"

Some part of me knew the buttons I'd need to push to expose her insecurities and turn the issue around. This casual cruelty sometimes appeared during my manic episodes and was in full effect at this moment. Suddenly I'd made her seem like the attacker.

Vanya was taken aback, unsure what had sparked the anger or raised voice. "I didn't mean anything by it. I was just..."

I cut her off. "If you have a problem with me, just say it. Don't dance around the issue." At the time, I had no idea how intimidating or threatening I could be, so when Vanya began to cry and pack her travel bags for a second time, I figured we were done. I lashed out again. "So, you're going back to your parents?"

Vanya just cried, packed a few of her clothes as fast as she could, then ran upstairs and out of the basement. Although Vanya had received permission to live at my house, she had not been entirely truthful about our living situation. Due to her parents' strong religious beliefs, they were quite upset when they found out that we were living in the same room. I never knew it was an issue until later that week.

Two days after she left, I received a call from Vanya explaining that she would move out unless I proposed. I had scared her, but for some reason, she had forgiven me and her parents were demanding that we either live apart or move forward. I had never taken ultimatums well and, without thinking, I hung up the phone and stormed downstairs. Anger overtook me. I was unable to remember any good things about our relationship, so I grabbed her things and threw them into the center of the room. As the phone continued to ring, I ignored it until all of Vanya's belongings were packed. I finally answered the phone, but only after I was done. Vanya was sobbing.

"I'm sorry, I had to tell my parents. I didn't know what to do and I was going to tell you, but you seemed so angry. Can you forgive me, and can we move on?" Vanya asked with a pleading tone.

Like always, I was reacting to the present, unable to separate reality from my swirling emotions. "No," I said, my voice cold and decisive, "I can't. You made your choice." After all the times Vanya had forgiven me, I didn't even consider her feelings or point of view. "Your stuff is packed, and you can pick it up tomorrow." With that I hung up the phone without a second thought. When the phone began to ring again, I leaned down and tore the phone cable out of the jack, tearing the drywall in the process. I had truly cared for her, but I was unable to see beyond the moment I was in. Also, my twisted version of the events made me believe that Vanya had betrayed me. My mind was made up. Like in the elevator, like my initial meeting with Doctor Smith, I had no control and there was no way I would consider taking Vanya back. Again, my broken mind with its twisted realities had ruined another relationship, but I was unaware and uncaring. It would take years to be able to look back and see how harsh I could be.

Each and every woman I had dated deserved better than I was capable of providing. I wasn't inherently evil or even a bad guy, but my moods and changing views of the world around me made me erratic, irrational and often mean. Although I was, at times, a good boyfriend, my sharp tongue had not been dulled by the multitude of medications I was taking and although I was never physically abusive, my explosions always terrified those closest to me.

Although Vanya did call a few more times, I never spoke with or saw her again. What impacts me now is that even after ending one of my most serious relationships I didn't feel any regret, pain or sadness. Later that week, I was given a higher daily dose of Lithium and started on another drug called

Lamictal. My doctor and family were trying desperately to find something to help stabilize me. I knew nothing would work because I still didn't believe anything was wrong with me. Not only did I hate taking the medications, but the medications became a scapegoat. For me, the fact that I was still having problems even while taking the medications proved that my problems were the result of the world around me and not due to any mental disorder.

Two weeks after breaking up with Vanya and starting yet another medication, now taking even more medications than before, my swings continued to worsen. There were very brief moments when my family saw a flash of the real person I was and the potential I had, but those fleeting moments only brought my family a false sense of hope that always left them disappointed.

Mania had awoken again. Although my breakup should've affected me to some degree, my mania wouldn't allow introspection, and certainly wouldn't permit feeling down. As it entered the second stage I found my way back down to Denver and its many bars and clubs. The risks I took, whether talking about casual romantic encounters or my use of illicit drugs, had become more perilous and daring than ever before. Taking 1800 milligrams of Lithium, 450 of Lamotrigine and four milligrams of Clonazepam per day should've made it hard for me to even get out of bed, but my mania was stronger than ever.

On that Friday I was at one of my favorite clubs drinking when I saw one of my best friends. I had known Ming since the sixth grade, and we had always been very close. Since he still lived in the mountains where we had both grown up, I was surprised to have run into him and was glad to see him. Unlike me, he didn't drink or do drugs, nor ever had. The only reason he ever came to clubs was to relax, socialize and blow off some stress that came with running his family's restaurant.

Since I had gotten to the club early, I had been able to secure a small table. I called out and waved to get his attention and was delighted at the look of surprise on his face. Most of my close friends had no idea of how I spent my manic weekends, so I understood why he looked surprised to see me waving him over. "Ming, get over here!"

Ming had been born in Hong Kong and was the only one in his family that spoke, wrote and read his native tongue fluently. It was partly the reason he was placed in charge of his family's two restaurants. The real reason, however, was that Ming was a stand-up guy. Always well dressed and mature, Ming couldn't even swear without it sounding strange.

He grinned and made his way through the crowd toward me. We had been the best of friends in middle school but had drifted apart slightly during high school. Not because we had a falling out, but because even in high school my bipolar had begun to take over, and Ming just didn't understand my erratic mood swings. Like always, he was overdressed for the club, wearing slacks, polished black shoes and a nice jacket that screamed money, but I had always liked that Ming knew who he was and didn't care what others thought. As he approached the small table I was sitting at, I stood up and shook his hand. "It's good to see you. What in the world are you doing down in Denver without calling me?" I asked while motioning for him to sit down.

Ever since we had graduated from high school I had been trying to convince Ming to get out of the mountains and away from his restaurants. He had expressed interest in going to college and he was certainly smart enough to do more with his life. Although Ming had told me that he wasn't happy, I knew he would never move forward with his own life until he was sure that his family would be successful without his aid.

Something felt different about him. "I tried giving you a call, but you never pick up," Ming answered. "I wanted to let you know that we sold the restaurants and I'm going to be applying to The University of Colorado."

"That's great. Let me buy you a drink in celebration."

"Thanks, but I'm okay. Just here to dance and have some fun." Although I went to clubs to drink and flirt, Ming had always been able to have fun without the aid of alcohol or drugs. He was one of the more secure men I knew.

"So when are you moving down here?"

Ming shrugged. "I'm actually trying to figure that out. I need to find a place to rent."

"No way!" I grinned. "There is no way you're renting when we have plenty of room at my house. Can you handle sleeping on a futon?" The idea of having one of my best friends as a roommate sounded perfect to me.

"What about you and Vanya?" Ming asked. "I thought she was living with you?"

"That's over," I said casually. "For the best, for sure."

"You broke up?" Ming looked surprised, not only at the news, but at how nonchalant I seemed. "What happened? The last I heard was that you two were getting serious."

I shrugged. "Some things just end."

"All of your relationships end." Ming tried to smile but was unable to hide his concern. I didn't mind; he was kind to ask, but at this point nothing could've gotten me down. "Are you okay?"

I lifted a shot of tequila into the air, I laughed and nodded. "Same shit, different day." With that I tossed back the tequila. Ming still appeared troubled. Biting down on the lemon to chase the shot, I added: "Seriously, bro, I'm good. It was never going to work."

"Well, for what it's worth, I'm sorry."

"You're a good guy, Ming," I said with a chuckle before asking: "So you think you can live with me as a roommate?"

"Probably not," Ming chuckled, "but if it's okay with your family, I can certainly give it a try."

I laughed, knowing that my entire family viewed Ming more as my brother than a friend. "You are family," I said, then waved down the waitress to order another shot. "Seriously, we'd love to have you."

Ming nodded. "Well then, I'll give your parents a call so we can work out the details."

"So, do we have a deal?" I asked, and offered up my hand. When he shook my hand and nodded, I laughed. "We're going to have a blast. Promise." Had Ming been aware of the person I had become, he would've run out of that club without looking back. Over the next few months, Ming quickly learned why all my relationships were doomed to collapse. Not even one of my most prized friendships was safe.

PART THREE: THE END OF DENIAL

I. BIPOLAR UNMASKED

A week after Ming moved into the basement, my mania was still in charge. Although I had no idea, during the past month my mania had been growing ever more intense. Since I only socialized when in a manic stage, Ming never thought my behavior was odd. In the second stage of my mania, I was gone most nights, drinking, socializing and hitting harder drugs as I continued to slip further from reality. Like always, Ming quickly found a job and therefore avoided seeing the dangerous risks that became more radical and life-threatening with each passing night. He knew I drank and partied, but only Mike and a few of Mike's friends knew how hard.

To me, the risks I took, whether drugs, one-night stands or fights, were simply fun. I was my most charming and likable during my early manic stages, attracting good girls and friends, but as my mania grew more intense, everything changed. Not only did I take greater risks, but the drugs were harder, and my circle of friends changed dramatically. Near the end of the month, after getting home after a long night of drinking and socializing, Ming walked into the kitchen, catching in the midst of me taking my medications.

When I noticed him standing there, shock and denial began to war, and my mind raced for the most plausible lie. Ming pointed to the handful of pills I still needed to take. "Are you sick?" Ming asked, his eyes moving from my handful of pills to my eyes. "Why are you taking all those pills?"

"It's medication for my ADD," I lied, surprised at how quickly I had come up with a perfect explanation. Due to all of the precarious situations I always found myself in, my ability to lie had become imperative to my survival, especially with some of the individuals I was partying with. One huge problem with lying was that it had become more comfortable than telling the truth. Worse was the fact that I could actually believe the lies I told. Although I was taking my medications every day, my mind was slipping further away from what most people would consider normal. Not that I noticed or cared.

Unfortunately, my father had just refilled my ADD medication and it was sitting on the counter next to Ming. As smart as he was, he looked at my hand and then at the prescription before gently prying. "That's a ton of pills." Ming was a smart guy. He knew I was aware he had caught my lie, but he didn't press as he sat down at the kitchen table, speaking as if nothing was different. "I just got a call from Albert and he wants to go out to celebrate his birthday. He was wondering if you and I wanted to meet him at Market." Market was one of my favorite clubs down in Denver with great music, a large dance floor and great drinks, so I was certainly up for going out. Had I understood my moods, I would never have exposed Ming to my manic side, but I was just excited to hang out with Ming and Albert.

"Sounds good. When does he want to go?"

"He was thinking Friday night," Ming responded before taking a sip of his orange juice. "I thought we should invite your sister, just so she can get out and relax."

Chandi had just had a bad breakup with a boyfriend that had never been right for her and Ming was right, she did need some relaxation. My sister had grown up around so much chaos, she always dated men that kept that chaos in her life, a fact that I know I am partially, if not fully, responsible for. Ming had a good point. I nodded. "I bet she'd love to come. Let me confirm with her, but you can tell Albert that we'll see him there."

Friday came and, as always, Ming was happy to be the designated driver. My sister had to be up early the next day but that was fine with Ming and me. I was itching for something to do and really didn't care if we had to leave early or not as long as I got my fill of adventure. With the three of us in Ming's nice car, we headed down to Denver. On the drive I was on a roll with jokes and wit, keeping my sister and Ming laughing as the sun tucked down behind the mountains to our backs.

When we arrived at the club, Albert was waiting for us. After paying to get in, Ming and my sister were wishing Albert a happy birthday while I walked straight for the bar. The long, oval bar was at the center of the club with three to six bartenders working at any given time. Since we had arrived early, I was able to walk right up and order. When the only male bartender came over, I seized my chance. "Four shots of tequila, please. Two for me and two for my friend's birthday."

"Sure thing. You want to start a tab?"

"Sure." The four shots were poured and on the table before I even had my credit card in hand. The bartender took my card wordlessly and moved onto the next customer.

The night was just beginning, and I was looking forward to some real fun, so I tossed back the first shot and then waved Albert over. I caught the bartender's eye as he came by and motioned for one more. He quickly poured the shot with a quick flick of his wrist. "I'll keep them coming if you want?"

"Sounds like a plan," I said, before handing him a generous tip. Albert had already seen me and was walking towards the bar. I raised both glasses and waited for him to get close enough to hand him the drink before saying, "Here's to having a wild birthday."

Albert was a great guy and although he wasn't into drugs he did drink, which was nice since neither my sister nor Ming did. I had been out drinking with strangers the last few nights, given that my circle of friends had been shrinking in the last few years, so it was fun to have a good friend to share some drinks with. "Cheers," Albert said. We clinked glasses and tossed back our shots. I was ready for some fun, so I picked up the second shot for Albert and my third with a slight grin on my face. Albert was still chasing the drink with a lemon, and noticed I was holding a second shot for him. Laughing, he took the shot and said, "So you weren't kidding about the wild birthday?"

"I never kid about fun," I said before adding, "Should we get a table?" There weren't many tables as it was more of a dance club, but since we had arrived early, there were a few open.

"If you want," Albert said. I hoped my third shot would kick in shortly.

The strange thing about my mania was that the faster my mind was moving, the slower everything else felt. People around me seemed to be moving in slow motion while the music pumping through the speakers felt off and lazy. I was completely unaware that I felt any different than earlier that day, but my mind was ramping up. The shots were a vain attempt to slow my racing mind, or speed up the lagging surroundings, or align the two somehow. It never worked. I never stopped trying.

I didn't know it then, but I was trying to medicate myself with alcohol. As my emotions roared through me, I wasn't even thinking. I raised my hand and signaled the bartender for refills more as a reflex than anything else. Luckily, this wasn't the club where I had lost my cool and thrown a mug. Generally, the bartenders at Market were great and always gave a generous pour.

The night was no different for me and although I didn't know it, my view of the moment was always a reflection of my current moods. If I had a horrible time the previous night, I wouldn't have even remembered. My focus was always on the moment. Especially during my manic episodes where everything was focused on having fun and self-medicating, though I didn't know I was doing that at the time.

For the briefest moment, I realized that I didn't even remember what I had done the previous weekend. Not because of my medications, drugs or booze, but because I never looked back or forward. My future was the same way, but as quickly as I felt a slight realization, it was gone and forgotten. It was almost as if the bipolar was protecting me from seeing the devastation I always left in my wake or the bridges I burned that led to my dreams. Although I didn't even realize the small revelation I had, I know that this strange inability to see beyond my current mood was not unique to me. In fact, nearly every bipolar individual I have spoken with has expressed the same sensation of being a slave to their instant swings, unable to grasp the impact of their decisions or look back with a clear mind to learn from past mistakes. Had I not been intoxicated by my mania, I would have known that three shots of tequila was more than enough for starting the night out.

When the bartender handed me two more shots, I downed both and ordered a Long Island for myself. I was quickly growing more restless and was hoping to numb my mind in order to enjoy the night. Of course, alcohol and drugs were never the answer, but the drive for them was always there during these times.

I don't know how I avoided addiction, but I believe that because I was unable to function when my depression set in that kept me from forming steady habits. In short, the sword cut both ways. It is also worth mentioning that drugs and alcohol, besides being ineffective at calming my mind, were also extremely expensive. Within a span of ten minutes I had spent nearly eighty dollars on drinks. Without having, or being capable of holding a job, I was quickly building up a debt that I wouldn't be able to climb out of.

Albert downed his second shot and quickly put a lime in his mouth to smooth the burn. After throwing the lime out, Albert set down the shot glass and smiled. Unlike Ming, Albert was a big guy. Although he was short, he was stocky and had plenty of muscle. He and I had spent more than a few nights drinking together, so he wasn't surprised to see me drinking so heavily.

After coughing from the burn the alcohol had caused, Albert patted my shoulder and said, "It's great to see you, bro. I really appreciate you and Ming helping me celebrate in style."

"It's the least we could do," I responded while looking through the thickening crowd to find Ming and my sister. I spotted them out on the small balcony, enjoying the warm night at a small table they had snagged. "Shall we go sit with Ming and my sister?"

Albert couldn't hear me as the music of the club pounded loudly, the base hitting my body and making it difficult for us to hear each other. Instead of answering me, he just nodded and made for the balcony where Ming and my sister were waiting.

When we arrived at the small table I tried to sit down and relax, but the harder I tried to calm my mind the more it seemed to race out of control. My ability to focus was now non-existent. Worse still was the restlessness that I felt. As Albert, Ming and Chandi talked, I tried to pay attention, but eventually my need to move overwhelmed me. I stood and excused myself. The quickly growing crowd on the dance floor was my destination. Typically, I didn't like to dance, but at the moment I was drawn to any activity that would either keep me distracted from my own thoughts or help burn what felt like an eternal spring of energy.

The pulse of the music was enjoyable as I danced, each beat striking my body, daring me to stop. Although I wanted to dance, I was still holding my drink. As more people moved onto the dance floor, I decided to look for a place to set down my glass. I spotted a table of three girls looking at me and giggling. I walked over. All three women were pretty, but one girl stood out among her friends. She was wearing a silky gray dress that caught my attention. She had curly black hair that fell down her cheeks, framing her heart-shaped face and dark hazel eyes. The three girls blushed when they noticed me approaching, acting like they hadn't seen me at all. I figured they had just noticed how bad a dancer I was, but that didn't bother me.

Like most times when my mania was threatening to peak, I was bold and fearless. My mania had always made approaching women easier for me, but only when it was growing out of control. When I arrived at the table, I gave a gentle smile, leaned in so that the girls could hear me and asked: "Can I buy you ladies a drink?" The girls nodded, so I smiled and reached out my hand to introduce myself. "I'm Kirk, it's nice to meet you all." The girl in the gray dress fess my main focus. "Was my dancing really bad, or do I have hope?"

All three girls laughed, instantly relieving any tension they might have felt. The black-haired woman reached out and shook my hand. "My name is Sara and no, your dancing wasn't bad." Sara's smoky eyes were kind, and she pointed to a chair. "You can sit down if you want?" I didn't want to sit, but I wanted another drink and Sara had caught my attention, so I pulled up a barstool and joined them.

After ordering all the girls a drink and enjoying a few laughs, I looked at Sara and stood up, offering my hand. "I'm still in the mood to dance if you are up to it." I was usually not such a forward guy, but out of all the bad that came with mania, confidence and lack of fear were two perks that I did enjoy.

Sara took my hand, and I nodded to her friends before leading her onto the dance floor. The restlessness I felt had not faded, but being out on the dance floor helped, as did having someone to dance with. As the music pulsed through the dance floor, Sara put her arms around my neck and pulled me closer. All the alcohol I had downed that night was beginning to kick in, but for some reason it was hard to feel or enjoy. I certainly wasn't feeling any more relaxed. However, I was enjoying my time with Sara. Although I was having a hard time focusing, Sara and I were hitting it off.

"How about we take a break?" Sara asked when the song we were dancing to ended. I nodded, so she took my hand and led me off the dance floor. I expected to head back towards her friends, but Sara led me to a different table where she sat down. "I'm up for another cocktail if you are?"

I sat down and smiled. "Sure thing. What do you want?"

It was then that Sara leaned forward and kissed me. Her forward behavior was shocking, to say the least. After a long, soft kiss, she whispered in my ear, "My place isn't far away, and I've had a rough week. Would you like to ditch this place and have a cocktail where we can talk?"

I had always taken foolish chances when it came to matters of the fairer sex and I was about to say yes when Albert came over. The alcohol that still wasn't silencing my thoughts had hit my friend hard as he leaned on the table, nearly slipping off as he tried to stay on his feet. Puffing out his chest, Albert leaned towards Sara and said, "Aren't you a beautiful little lady."

Although Albert was a good guy, I could tell that his swaying and slurred speech were bothering Sara. Acting fast, I introduced them to each other.

"Albert, this is Sara and Sara, this is my good friend Albert who's celebrating his birthday tonight and doing a good job from what I can tell."

Sara let down her guard. She gave him a polite, cool smile. Behind that smile, I could tell she was not pleased that we had been interrupted. "Happy birthday, Albert. If you don't mind, I," before Sara could finish, Albert sat down between us. Annoyed but not put off entirely, Sara stood up and straightened her short gray dress before walking to my side. Leaning forward to reach the Cosmopolitan I had ordered for her, she kissed my cheek and said, "When you're ready to go, just come and get me." With that, she kissed me once more and walked away as Albert stared at me.

"You dog!" Albert said, playfully hitting my shoulder. "I still say she'd be kissing me if I had seen her first."

I just laughed, not willing to pass up such an invitation. I was about ready to go and tell Ming I didn't need a ride home when my mania ratcheted up another notch. Suddenly, my restlessness turned into a light paranoia. There were a group of guys standing behind Albert, and although I know now that they were simply hanging out, at the time I felt like they were watching me. I hadn't even noticed Albert was still talking when I stood up, glaring at one of the guys that had looked my way. Lifting up my hands, I shouted, my words faint against the booming music that was making my ears ring. "You have a problem with me?"

The guy I was addressing tried his best to ignore me, but that wasn't going to work. "What's wrong, bro?" Albert asked as I stood there staring.

"I'm just sick of that guy glaring at me."

"What are you talking about, bro? Just relax."

I couldn't relax. The mania in me knew the guy had a problem with me and I had an overwhelming sense that I might need to protect myself. Usually, I could have blamed this aggressive behavior on alcohol, but these same feelings had happened multiple times when I was completely sober. The impulse to fight was always the same when caused by my mania and it made me a dangerous person with no one being able to read my next action. Not only was I completely out of touch with anything but my immediate judgments, but because I lacked the ability to see my situation clearly, I was unable to recognize that the guy I was threatening was not alone.

The anger I felt was hot and the fact that I felt more and more eyes turning towards me and judging me certainly didn't help. I felt indestructible, ready for a confrontation, but just as I was walking past

Albert to confront the guy I was looking at, Albert caught my arm and held me back.

"Dude, it's my birthday. Settle down. Besides, he's got at least six friends, not that I wouldn't back you up, but I'm a bit drunk."

I was breathing heavily, and even Albert seemed hesitant to hold me back, but as the guys at the next table began to stand up in preparation for a confrontation, my sister and Ming walked over. Ming and Chandi had no idea that I was near blowing a gasket, which was probably lucky. She inserted herself into a potentially explosive situation without realizing and leaned forward. "I need to leave soon. Is that okay with you?"

The tone of my sister's voice was so gentle that most of the anger I was feeling faded for the moment. At least I had not hit my peak yet, as once I was fully manic and had a goal in mind, there was nothing that could calm me or keep me from acting.

"Do you mind if I dance a bit longer?" I asked and my sister nodded.

"Not at all. Ming and I will be waiting at the front. Is thirty minutes enough?"

I wanted to say no, but I needed to catch up with Sara before I knew what I would do. I nodded. Even with as much alcohol as I had consumed, I still didn't feel drunk. I was beginning to feel relaxed, but that didn't mean that I was in control. "Okay," I said, heading off into the crowd.

After losing track of time the second time my sister found me her tone had changed and I could tell she was upset. "It's been nearly forty-five minutes."

"I'm sorry. I have to catch up with someone and might not need a ride home. Can you give me fifteen more minutes?"

As always, I was being selfish, but my sister nodded. "Come tell us as soon as you know, okay?"

"Deal," I said, not wasting time as I moved into the crowd looking to find Sara before leaving. I hadn't seen her in a while and was wondering if she had left, but finally I found Sara sitting and laughing with her friends near the back of the club. When Sara saw me, she smiled and stood up to great me. I wanted to stay, but I had promised my sister and knew that Ming was also waiting for me. "So, Kirk, I thought you had vanished without saying goodbye."

"I want to stay, but everyone is bugging me to leave. I wouldn't go, but my sister is here and it's my friend's birthday. Can I give you a call sometime?"

Sara took a pen out of her small wrist purse and leaned away and over the table, writing her number on a napkin before handing it to me. "Call me tomorrow, okay?" As I reached for the napkin, she pulled it just out of my reach and put one hand on my chest, meeting my eyes with hers. "I like you, so don't play any games."

"Tomorrow," I said as she handed me the number. I leaned in and gave her a quick kiss on the cheek before turning away and moving towards the club's exit. Although I had enough energy to dance until dawn, I figured the night had been successful. Also, once we dropped off my sister, there were also good clubs in Boulder if Ming was okay driving.

I met up with my sister and Ming, we all wished Albert a happy birthday, and Ming made sure that Albert had a safe ride home before we left the club and parted ways. After leaving the walk back to the car felt like a one-sided conversation as I teased my sister for needing to be up early. I wasn't aware that both Ming and Chandi were upset with me.

When we got into the car and began our trip home, my hope of enjoying the rest of the evening was quickly shattered as my sister scolded me. "You knew I had to be up, and it is three hours later than you promised we would leave."

The rage was always on deck. I immediately lashed out with a violent tone and harsh language. "You didn't even have to fucking come if you had to be up so damned early. Shit, Ming and I only invited you out of pity." As always, I had a way of honing in on someone's insecurities or pain so that my verbal attacks were more effective.

Ming jumped in, his voice calm as he talked to my sister. "That isn't true, Chandi. Kirk, you owe your sister an apology!"

"So you two are ganging up on me?" My mania had finally peaked, and I didn't see my sister or one of my longest and best friends. Instead I saw enemies who had me cornered in a car. Taken over by roaring emotions fed by a thick river of energy, I felt trapped and attacked. The curse words I used and the way I yelled brought my sister to tears and caused Ming to yell back. I had never seen Ming yell, so it only added to my delusional idea that they were both against me.

"Calm down, damn it!" Ming shouted as I began hitting his dashboard as hard as I could, but there was no chance that anyone could reason with me. When I began to try and unlock the door and open it while we were driving on the highway, my sister began to panic.

I didn't hear what she said, but Ming continued to relock the doors and attempt to drive as I hit the windows, cursed and threatened both Ming and my sister. For me, the twenty-minute drive felt like an eternity and I just wanted out of the car, even if that meant breaking down the door.

"Let me out!"

"Fine," Ming said with disgust, slowing the car and beginning to pull over.

Not wanting me stranded on the side of the road, my sister protested. "Please don't pull over. Let's just get home." My sister's sobs were enough to state how the evening had turned, but I was like a wild animal, unable to control my mouth or actions. I continued to say everything I could that would hurt both Ming, one of my best friends, and Chandi, the sister that had always been there for me.

We finally arrived home. I surged out of the car and charged into the house, slamming every door I passed and cursing loud enough to wake our neighbors. My parents rushed down to see what was wrong, but I had already grabbed the portable phone, gone into the basement and out the back door. Our house backed an open space, so I quickly jumped the back fence and kept dialing Mike. I wanted to be as far from my sister and Ming as possible, even when they hadn't done anything wrong. My actions and thoughts were not rooted in any normal reality, to say the least.

I hopped the fence in our backyard while dialing Mike to come and pick me up. The instinct to flee and the anger I felt were overwhelming. My outburst had been the most violent and aggressive that I had ever had, and I was on multiple medications that were supposed to help keep me from such explosions. Unfortunately, I was totally out of control, unable to see or care how I was acting, and I truly felt like my actions had been justified.

I walked for hours. Meanwhile my family desperately looked for me and called the police. I was paranoid enough to avoid any cars that were out driving which is probably the only reason I avoided being arrested that night. I was wild, angry and have no doubt that I would have attacked anyone who came near me, cop, friend or foe.

After a few hours of walking, my mania vanished and once again I was plunged into a deep and heavy depression. For me and many others with bipolar, the change from depression to mania is a slower process, but that was not the case when swinging the other way. The sudden shift, the depression, the night's activities, or some combination of the three left me exhausted, and though I was still filled with anger, I had the presence of mind to sneak into the house and climb into bed. My swings were getting worse and it didn't appear that all the medications I was taking were helping. A multitude of factors were at play, involving the drugs and alcohol, the prescription meds, my diet, and whatever mix of hormones my body was creating, whether correctly or not. None of that could explain why I would become so manic when completely sober.

Amazingly enough, the next morning, Ming came into my room. "Listen, Kirk, I'm really sorry about how everything went down last night." Although my depression was holding strong, it was still in the beginning stages, so I was actually able to make eye contact. What strikes me as strange now is that I remember not knowing why Ming was sorry. It was as if the previous night had been a dream. I remembered all the details of the night, for I hadn't had enough to drink to change that, however, my view of what happened was based on the current moment.

I spoke quietly; I was in no mood for talking. "No problem, bro. I'm sorry too. Let me get some sleep and we'll talk later." There was no reason Ming should've been the one to apologize. He might have felt like he and Chandi had ended my fun, but that in no way excused my behavior later, and as always the bipolar had blocked out any iota of empathy or real introspection.

After the wild night, my family felt obligated to explain to Ming that I had been diagnosed with bipolar and that I hadn't been myself the previous night. As I would've expected from Ming, he never treated me differently. He did, however, move out a few months later for his own personal reasons. Ever since that night, Ming's eyes were open to what bipolar really was, admitting that before seeing it with his own eyes, he had always thought of bipolar as a simple and harmless disorder. I lost many friends because of bipolar, but luckily Ming is still one of my closest friends. I never did call Sara, and that was not the last bridge I burned.

II. THE BEST GIFT BIPOLAR EVER GAVE ME

During that summer, I had a total of three major episodes, two manic and one depressive. The outburst that had rocked my friendship with Ming had sent me into a deep depression that lasted nearly a month. Dr. Smith was trying his best, but I heard him tell my mother that we had tried nearly everything and that she needed to adjust to the idea that I could continue to get worse. In the end, my family and Dr. Smith both felt like I was my most stable on Lithium and Lamictal. Although the Lamictal had begun to cause short term memory loss while the Lithium destroyed my thyroid, thinned my hair and dulled my mind, the combination of the two drugs was still the best we had found. I did slightly object to how everyone else defined 'doing well.' To me it appeared, and to be honest, I still feel this way, that as long as I was heavily drugged and not causing immense problems, then I was considered to be doing well. The only problem was that I wasn't getting better, my mind felt slow and even though the medications did occasionally slow down how often I swung from mania to depression, it didn't make the swings any better.

As the summer was coming to a close and I was coming out of one of my darkest depressions, I stumbled across one of my old crushes. Nicoal was a beautiful Korean girl that I had liked since I was a senior and she was a freshman in high school. She had graduated and was now eighteen, so I asked her out on a date.

I took her out to a restaurant and found her just as I remembered from a few years ago. Nicoal was young and naive, not really aware that she was on an official date just as I was unaware that she was currently involved with someone. Amazingly, even though we had no idea of each other's intentions, I found talking with her was easy and relaxing. I had dated some wonderful women, but Nicoal was a new experience and the connection we had was so much more than physical.

After an enjoyable meal, it was time for her to go home. Unfortunately for the both of us, I was in the first stage of my mania. I knew it would be the last time I saw her that summer, and inhibitions had never been present whenever mania had a hold of me, and while I should have stopped myself, there's no undoing the past. I suddenly reached out, pulled her close and kissed her. At first, she melted into my arms before she stiffened up. The kiss had been amazing.

The next day she called me. "We need to talk." She came across as unexpectedly harsh, and I couldn't figure out why.

"Okay," I responded slowly, "what do we need to talk about?"

"You were completely out of line last night."

"What?"

Nicoal sounded flustered as she explained herself. "You didn't even ask if I was dating someone, yet you had the audacity to kiss me. Why would you..."

I cut Nicoal off before she could continue. "I am so sorry. I just felt we connected..." I answered honestly. "Are you seeing anyone? If so, I apologize."

"I'm leaving for college, so no, I'm not in a relationship, but you caught me off guard." There was a pause before Nicoal added, "I'm not saying that I didn't enjoy it, but still."

Nicoal was younger than I and had not dated much. I realized that, given our vast difference in experience, I probably did surprise her, and perhaps not in a good way. Not wanting to lose my chance with her, I quickly added, "You have every right to still be mad at me, but I had a great time and wouldn't have done that if I had known." As I spoke, I was fairly certain that I would've kissed her regardless of her situation. There was a heat there that I couldn't explain. It was intoxicating and I liked her. The kiss had been amazing, making it all the more bitter-sweet because she was heading off to college in Florida later that week.

I heard her sigh on the other end of the line before speaking again. "I also had a great time. I leave in a few days, but maybe we can catch up next summer."

Yeah right, I thought. I was certain right that moment that long-distance relationships didn't work, and regardless, we didn't even have a true relationship. But I responded with as much cheer as I could muster. "Until next summer."

"You could always email me?"

"I will do that." Nicoal was young and a bit immature, but she had a great mind, a glowing personality and she was beautiful. The only hesitation I had was knowing that I really did like her and in a way I wasn't familiar with.

To my surprise, we did stay in touch. There were lapses when I was depressed and never checked my email, but overall, we talked once every week or so. Since we weren't exclusive I continued to go out when my mania took over. Neither of us knew if she was even going to come back, so I would occasionally find myself enjoying short romances. What was odd was that I would often think of Nicoal after ending a relationship. Even my serious relationships had never held my attention the way Nicoal did. I wasn't sure if it was the idea of Nicoal or that we had a true spark.

Although my romantic endeavors didn't seem to change, my willingness to try more intense and serious drugs had changed. My manias had spiraled out of control so badly that I often thought my head would explode. This feeling made me seek out stronger drugs and eventually I found a few that were hard enough to quiet my mind for a few hours. They did nothing to improve my manic peaks, but they were powerful enough to provide me a few hours of respite from my own mind, which is why I was drawn to them. As I said before, I have no doubt that my depressions and my inability to function during my deepest downs saved me from becoming a junkie. Had I been able to continue using, I doubt I would still be alive.

As the year went on I continued to deteriorate, but I tried my best to email Nicoal when I was functioning. I had been treating my bipolar for over a year, but nothing had helped the overall condition. In fact the intensity of the peaks and depressions, if anything, worsened. My depressions were bad enough that I was unable to even attend my college classes. My sister and mother actually had to help me drop out of college just to keep me from getting F's in every class. Before that year, I had still been able to function, but my life was rapidly slipping beyond any semblance of normal.

For many people suffering with bipolar, the medications do take away their intoxicating highs or make them feel sluggish or sick, so many psychiatrists struggle with keeping their patients on the medications. I fully admit that I wanted to stop, but I had promised my mother that I wouldn't. My irrational idea of honor was the only thing that kept me on my meds. Although I hated my medications, I do believe things would have become much worse had I not continued taking the meds. To anyone reading this, I feel I must say that listening to my doctors did save my life.

On Valentine's Day that year I had no date and had cycled back into another depression. When I received a cute card from Nicoal, I wasn't even able to email and thank her. Even though the card had not magically pulled me out of a depression it did make me feel better. Over the next three months, I had a few weeks when I was somewhat normal. My family actually dreaded these times of normality even more than my swings, mostly because they had no way of knowing what might trigger a depressive or manic state. Living with me must have been like trying to run a sprint while holding nitroglycerine. My family never knew when I would explode.

When I received an email from Nicoal telling me that she was flying back to Colorado to work during her summer vacation, I was eager to see her and was just beginning to enter my first and most mild stage of mania. I called her two days after she had returned, pleased to catch her on the phone. "Hi Nicoal, it's Kirk. I was wondering if you wanted to get together in the next few days." I didn't know why I felt nervous calling, but she sounded pleased to hear from me.

"I wish I could, but I have to work." After I asked when she had time and she responded with, "I'm really not sure." I was getting the idea that she wasn't interested, so I stopped calling.

Two weeks later, Nicoal called me, wondering why I hadn't called her. "You told me you would call me. It's been two weeks. What is going on?"

I was certainly surprised, for I had been sure she really wasn't interested. I was clear that Nicoal wasn't as experienced with dating as I thought I was. Surprised that she was interested, I quickly responded. "I'm sorry, but you seemed really busy and I didn't want to bother you." I had learned a while ago that pressuring a woman was the best way to push her away.

"I've been working two jobs, but I was still looking forward to seeing you. I even have today off."

"Okay then. How does dinner sound?" I asked.

"I don't have the car tonight, so I can't drive down to meet you."

"I'll drive up." I didn't want to miss my chance. "How about I pick you up at five?"

Nicoal sounded surprised but answered, "Okay. I'll see you then."

The moment I hung up the phone I rushed to get ready and clean up. Whenever I shaved, my mother knew that I wasn't depressed, but it still worried her as that usually meant the family was going to have to deal with some kind of manic outburst in the future.

I left a note for my family and headed out. When I picked up Nicoal, she was wearing a black dress decorated with a few sparkles. She was really tan from spending her time in Florida, but her black hair, gentle brown eyes and the dress matched her skin well. Unlike last time, we were both aware that this was an official date and for some reason things seemed harder than I remembered. After the dinner as we were walking back to the car, I was wondering if I had been wrong about the chemistry Nicoal and I had, but when we reached the car and I opened the door for her, she embraced me and pulled me in for a long kiss. Suddenly the sparks were back, and the tension was gone. We both had been trying to force things.

As my mania continued to intensify, Nicoal and I spent as much time as we could together. After only three weeks of dating, I knew I loved her. It wasn't the mania, although I believe I moved faster because of my mania, but the love I felt was warm and different. When the summer came to a close, I was foolish enough to go to a jewelry store, bringing in my own design for an engagement ring. My family liked Nicoal and everything seemed so easy, but I maxed out my credit card buying her a ring that I couldn't afford. Lost again in the manic present, I didn't wonder about Nicoal saying no to a marriage proposal. I just assumed she would say yes. Why wouldn't she? The fact she was only nineteen or that she was going back to Florida for school never even made me wonder.

When the summer was gone, I approached her parents to ask for their blessings because I was going to ask Nicoal to marry me. They were not entirely eager about the idea, but, even had they not given me their blessings, I would have asked her anyway. Out of all the times that bipolar had destroyed my relationships and left my life in ruins, I don't know if I would ever have asked a nineteen-year-old to marry me had I not been manic, especially when I had no degree or source of income. In this instant, my inability to separate my emotions from reality and logic led to the single greatest risk I would ever take.

III. CARING ENOUGH TO SEE THE TRUTH

When Nicoal left for Florida at the end of the summer we decided that we would remain exclusive. I had tried a long-distance relationship before, but this time I thought it could work. There is a very good reason that many long-distance relationships don't work out, but in our case, it was probably the best possible situation for the two of us, but most especially me.

First of all, Nicoal never saw me struggle, so her idea of me and the reality of who I was were very different from the truth. Not that I wanted to hide anything, but I still felt like I was fine and there was no need to scare Nicoal off with a story of me being bipolar. Secondly, I don't think she would ever agree to marry me had she seen how I really was. So in November of 2002, against everyone's advice and Dr. Smith's strong objections, I proposed.

Although her parents had given me their blessings they were worried about Nicoal making such a big decision at the age of nineteen. Had they known that I was neither financially or mentally stable, they would never have let their daughter marry me and I can't say that I would've blamed them. Luckily, however, nothing came up and Nicoal said yes.

After agreeing to marry me, Nicoal agreed to finish her associate's degree before moving back to Colorado to finish her schooling. While she was in town, everyone wanted to celebrate the good news, so Nicoal and I met her family up in Estes Park. Had I been able to sense my moods, I wouldn't have let myself be dragged there. My mania was gaining strength and I was already snappy, aggressive and out of sorts during the drive. At least when I was depressed, my family could claim that I was sick and resting. There was no way to explain or justify my manic outbursts or the dangerous paranoia. My actions were just too extreme to enable a plausible explanation, nor would I ever try or feel I needed to explain myself. I was, at the time, living in my own world.

Nicoal's mother kept asking if I was feeling well during our lunch at the Stanley hotel. She'd noticed my hands shaking. The tremors that were caused by my medications had grown worse, but I simply lied and said I must have had too much caffeine. Neither one of her parents seemed to buy my excuse, but they let it go. After lunch, Nicoal's mom wanted to go shopping and although I was beginning to feel anxious and a bit delusional, I couldn't say no.

When we arrived at the first store, I realized that I had forgotten my sunglasses at the hotel. They were expensive, so I was furious with myself. Nicoal, beautiful soul that she was, picked up that something was off, calmly walked over to me and touched my shoulder. "What is wrong, sweetie?"

"I left my glasses at the hotel," I said, full of disgust and anger. I didn't want to have to go back and look and also figured that someone had already taken them, so I saw no point in being anything but angry.

"Why don't we just go back and get them?" Nicoal's suggestion was simple, logical and it would've been easy, but I had slipped beyond seeing reason at that point.

"Someone probably already stole them or stepped on them. Besides, there is no way that we'll be able to find where I left them." Nicoal pulled me out of the store and away from her parents before I could really make a scene. She held my hand gently and guided me out to the street so we could talk.

"You don't need to yell."

"I can't believe you are giving me a hard time. I loved those glasses."

"So let's go get them?"

"I can't believe we have to drive back just because I forgot my glasses," to me, my anger and frustration made perfect sense, but to Nicoal, my reaction seemed more than odd.

"Are you feeling okay? Did my family upset you or something?" Nicoal was just trying to understand why I was growing so angry, but there was no way she could. No sane individual could fathom the swirling thoughts in my head, nor understand why such a small thing could cause so much rage.

"I'm feeling fine!" I shouted, making a few people walking by in the street stop in surprise. "No let go of me," I said harshly, tearing my hand from Nicoal's and confusing her even more. Although I wasn't aware at the time, I now realize that Nicoal had been extremely worried as she ran back inside the store. When she emerged I was already two blocks away, forcing her to run and catch up. Although that day and what happened is one of my worst memories, it is also the point in time when I can clearly see my life's path change. Sometimes it takes losing or nearly losing something very important to see the truth. For me, it was either losing Nicoal or coming to the end of my denial.

A steady stream of cursing came boiling out of me. I stomped along toward my parents' car and didn't really pay attention to Nicoal rushing to catch up with me.

"Kirk, I can just go get them, if you don't want to go back?" Nicoal was trying her best to remain calm. "Do you want me to drive?"

"Son of a..." I said, kicking a rock hard as I pulled out the keys to my dad's Passat and handed them to Nicoal. "I don't feel like driving."

No one deserved to be treated this way, least of all the woman I intended to marry, but such was the power of late-stage mania. Without the awareness of what I was doing, I had no idea how I was acting or talking, or who it might hurt.

Our path took us over a small bridge that spanned over a mountain river. Nicoal kept pressing me. "You're not acting like you're okay. Just tell me. Did I upset you, are you feeling alright?"

For some reason I just snapped, my voice booming into the mountain air as Nicoal's gentle question became a huge argument. I remember her shouting at me not to talk to her in such a way, but I was truly out of control. The exact contents of my mania-fueled tirade are lost to the heat of rage. I do remember cursing at everything, angry that I was in Estes Park, furious that I was out shopping, and livid that I had left my only good pair of sunglasses where someone could easily take them. In a word, I was mad.

"What is the problem?" a deep voice sounded from behind me. I whirled. A tall man in his late forties crossed the street, obviously worried about Nicoal with the way I was acting and shouting. The man was trying to do the right thing, but he had no idea what he was walking into.

All my fury was suddenly directed at the stranger as he tried to confront me. "I'm trying to have a conversation with my fiancé, if you don't mind."

"I do mind, and how dare..." the man was unable to finish. No, I'd snapped, grabbed him by his jacket and slammed him against the bridge's railing. I didn't see the fear in his eyes as I held him over a long drop into the rushing river below, but I'm sure he could see the anger in mine.

"You listen and listen carefully. Stay the hell out of my way and business." I added in a few expletives for good measure and was truly about to throw the guy off the bridge when Nicoal shouted for me to stop. For some reason, her voice cut through and I felt a wave of confusion. I let him go. The good Samaritan darted off, but the scene I had made had captured more attention than was favorable. Luckily Nicoal's parents were far enough away that they never knew what had happened. Nicoal wasn't the type to ask for help, but when I heard her calling my mother from our cell phone, explaining that something was wrong with me, I caught the slightest glimpse of horror in her eyes. There was no doubt that I loved Nicoal, but the look in her eyes made me wonder if she could ever see me the same again. My brief moment of clarity vanished, and I ran for the car, Nicoal following closely behind with tears streaming down while trying to talk to my mother.

I'd given her the keys; I couldn't get away. More than anything else I wanted to flee. Needed to flee. It was a small town and the police wouldn't stand for the way I had threatened a tourist, so I was eager to leave the scene as fast as possible. My reflection in the window was a bit surreal and too much for me to take, so I lashed out, hitting the window, luckily not hard enough to break it or my hand. Bravely, Nicoal walked slowly and carefully up to my side.

"Why don't we go for a short drive?" I didn't realize it at the time, but Nicoal was trying to get me out of the area as well, especially given the police sirens echoing through the small mountain town. My actions hadn't just horrified Nicoal, but everyone that had been watching. "I think we should go get your glasses," Nicoal said, a bit of panic in her voice.

Once the doors unlocked, I quickly entered the car and slammed the door as hard as I could. The impact shook the car and startled Nicoal, but I continued to lash out, reaching up and pulling down on the handle above the passenger side window until it snapped with a loud pop. Nicoal made a small squeak. Her tears thickened and began streaming down her beautiful cheeks.

"Let's go!" I demanded. Despite knowing I had hurt Nicoal in a way I might not be able to repair, I couldn't control myself. The realization only added to my anger, but then, for the very first time, I wondered if something might truly be wrong with me. I didn't want to feel angry or lash out and I certainly didn't want to hurt Nicoal, but I had, even if it hadn't been in a physical way.

There was something wrong with me. This realization dawned at long last. It had been glacially slow in coming, but it had finally arrived with chilling and inevitable certainty: the doctors were right. I was bipolar. I was bipolar and if I didn't do something, I was going to lose Nicoal.

Nicoal and her family didn't know what was wrong with me, and Nicoal still had the rest of the year to finish in Florida. As much as I hated admitting I wasn't entirely sane, or that the doctors were correct in their diagnoses, I hated the idea of losing Nicoal more.

Nicoal drove out of the parking lot and carefully avoided heading in the direction where I had physically assaulted a total stranger. Tears streamed down her cheeks, gathering at her small chin before falling to her lap. I just sat there staring at her, unable to control the rage and frustration consuming my thoughts. As I watched the tears roll down Nicoal's face, a single thought penetrated through my fog of rage. It was a brief thought and was quickly overshadowed by my mania, but I knew that if I couldn't find a way to control myself I was going to lose the woman I wanted to marry. That single thought is what propelled me to research bipolar and forever change my life. It was love that led me to the happiness and hope I now enjoy and is one of the many reasons I am now writing this memoir.

PART FOUR: RESEARCH AND DISCOVERY

:: When Madness Helps ::

I. TAKING ADVANTAGE OF MY MANIA

When I lost my mind in Estes Park, spewing hate-filled rhetoric and obscenities at the world, myself and the woman I wanted to marry, it was far from the first time my mania had overtaken my ability to think logically. Although I had nearly thrown a man off a bridge, it wasn't the worst thing I had done. I am horrified to think of the people I hurt during pointless fights, the damage I caused to property or all the times I awoke after taking a beating that I most surely deserved. Somehow, through some strange luck, I had always managed to avoid being arrested. There is little doubt that when my mania took over, I was little more than a rabid animal. When I lashed out, I was never aware of who I might be hurting or why. In truth, I thought I was protecting myself or acting as the situation demanded. Empathy for others was impossible. Like every outburst, I was always trapped in the present, my actions guided by my mania and the false realities it created.

What still startles me about Estes is that unlike most of my manic outbursts where I was unaware and uncaring of my actions, seeing the pain I had caused in Nicoal's gentle eyes had sent a ripple through my warped reality. Although it was only for a brief moment, it had allowed me, for the first time in my life, to see beyond the thick veil of denial that kept me from the truth. For a split second I had known something was wrong. Although that day remains one of my worst memories, it is also the day that changed my life in ways that I am finally able to describe.

No longer shielded by the denial that had kept me from committing to my therapy or even believing something might be wrong with me, it was the single threat of losing Nicoal that made me realize I had no choice but to change. The problem, however, was that even after glimpsing the truth of my situation for a brief moment, my bipolar was still in total control.

Coming to terms with my mental illness did not change the fact that there was no cure or that the massive amount of medication I was taking still couldn't calm the ferocity of my swings.

At first I had believed that knowing the truth might have offered me a chance to take control, but the fact that I didn't want to be depressed or manic did not enhance my ability to overcome whatever current episode I was entrenched in. Powerlessness overwhelmed me instead. I hated the world more than ever.

No one who suffers from bipolar wants to feel the dark and ominous depression that makes life feel heavy, tireless, and meaningless, nor do they enjoy the anxiousness, paranoia or delusions that accompany a manic episode. I was no different and it was one of the most frustrating aspects of bipolar. Not only did I now know that something was wrong, I had no ability to take control of my own mind, leaving me feeling powerless and trapped.

Although I hadn't been officially diagnosed until I was in college, it was becoming clear to me and my family that bipolar had long ago made me a passenger in my own life, not a pilot. Feeling like I was watching my life pass by instead of feeling or living it, life grew harder to take. I couldn't live like I was and although I was delusional at the time, I was determined to find a way to calm my wild mind.

That night after returning to Nicoal's house, she kept her distance from me, and I could hear her parents asking if everything was alright. Still feeling my mind racing, I wasn't about to go downstairs and eat with Nicoal's parents and sister as I could feel my mind racing out of control. When Nicoal came up, I was already in bed and she smiled at me. "Are you feeling better?"

"I'm fine," I responded. A response Nicoal hates to this day.

"Okay." She clearly didn't want to push talking about what had happened that day, not that I blamed her. "Good night," she added, kissing me on the cheek before crawling into bed next to me, wrapping her arms around me. Even then, I wanted to reach out and hold Nicoal, but I remained still and cold, staring up at the ceiling fan that spun slowly above the guest room's bed.

Nicoal fell asleep quickly while I, on the other hand, spent the night trying to slow down my racing mind. For a long while I thought about telling Nicoal that I was bipolar, but I was afraid of losing her. I also knew her parents wouldn't hear of their daughter marrying someone with bipolar, not that they would judge me, but I was well aware of how protective they were of their nineteen-year old daughter. Had they witnessed my actions in Estes, I don't know what they would've thought or done, but I do know that I would never have been able to fully gain their trust or love. It didn't take me long to decide that I wouldn't tell Nicoal. I would get better first and then tell her. It was a supremely selfish decision, but at the time I was still manic and unable to see how my actions could affect anyone other than me.

When I dropped Nicoal off at the airport the next day so that she could fly back to Florida and finish her semester she was wearing her ring with pride and smiling. I hadn't slept but didn't feel tired. Luckily my mania hadn't yet peaked, so my anger from the previous night had changed into plain energy that I released with constant conversation, jokes and teasing. Nicoal acted like my actions in Estes had simply been our first fight, kissing me and waving as she walked through security and away from my view. I didn't know until many months later that Nicoal had secrets of her own. She had grown up hard and had a past that no one would wish upon anyone, yet she was stronger for it. It was because she had been scarred by her past that we worked. Had she been as mentally strong as she is now I have no doubt she would've left me long before we ever exchanged vows. I owe Nicoal more than she'll ever know for sticking with me through some very rough times and am just glad we were able to heal together. Watching her leave was not hard on me, though I knew it should've been.

As I walked out of the airport and into the parking garage, I kept thinking about the first time I had met Dr. Smith. At the time, I hadn't cared about what he said, but now all I could remember was hearing him say that there was no cure and that I would, most likely, never lead a normal life. "He's wrong," I whispered under my breath. Since I had yet to reach my peak of my mania, I drove home, ready to prove the world wrong. I was willing to admit that something was wrong with my mind, but I wasn't ready to admit that I would never lead a normal life. I couldn't.

I barged into my house with a mission. My mother, pacing in front of the door, was worried after receiving the previous day's phone call from Nicoal. My little explosion in Estes had worried everyone, but my mom could tell I was on the move and simply let me head down to my room.

For the next week, I vanished in my room. I slept a few hours here and there, but I was lost in my research. The more I read about bipolar, the more the fog of denial continued to burn away. Like Dr. Smith had said, I had a 'textbook case' of bipolar I. What bothered me was that every blog, medical journal, book or memoir said that the key to treating bipolar was staying on medication. Not that I thought that was wrong, but the medications weren't curing my ills or making my swings better. I wanted a cure, but there was nothing I could find. After a week of researching every medication and treatment for bipolar disorder, my mania began to peak and my ability to research or focus with any guidance from reality or logic vanished. I shut off my computer rather than put my fist through it. I was now a bit delusional, swearing that everyone was wrong. There had to be a cure and I was determined to find it. Moreover, I believed I could actually do it. I didn't know that I would eventually stumble onto something that would forever change my life.

Most of my impossible missions, however, did not end with success.

I was a genius in my own mind, see. I knew secrets and had connected dots no one else could have possibly figured out. Now, after the fact, I feel quite comfortable calling myself a mad scientist. I had quite an elevated sense of my own abilities.

Unable to concentrate, I stood up and looked around my room that was littered with large stacks of printed articles, medical studies and medical journals that I highlighted and studied in a desperate attempt to find answers or holes that would lead me to an answer. When in my beginning two stages of mania, I became obsessed. My understanding of bipolar, the brain and the medications continued to deepen, and yet… The only problem was that everything I found pointed to the same answer: there was no cure.

Eventually, I had to research beyond the narrow scope of bipolar, still convinced that someone had missed something. It took me several years, but finally I believed I had stumbled onto a different avenue of looking at bipolar and its method of treatment. I never quit taking my medication, but I did begin experimenting on myself as only a madman would. There are reasons for the ethical and scientific guidelines that direct how medical studies and tests are performed, but I was not a doctor and I was hardly sane. Living in the present, desperate to find a cure while feeling indestructible, I took chances that nearly killed me.

Somehow, through a mixture of research, luck, and a mad man's willingness to risk life and limb on a hunch, no matter how scientifically based it was, is the basis for my success. As I discovered a new treatment that has led to my complete recovery and stunned my doctors it shows that there is always hope and there are always answers. The method I discovered has left me bipolar free for over four years and going. The best part is that with each passing day I've become ever more stable without the aid of any standard bipolar medications. I still seek regular help and I did not come off my meds until my doctor both knew what I was doing and slowly began to believe in it. I must say again that although I was foolish enough to experiment on myself, I do not condone any actions unless you are working with a medical professional. Whoever reads this must understand that changing medications or experimenting nearly killed me. I ended up lucky with the outcome, however, that is an unusual occurrence.

II. FAILING HEALTH AND THE CONTINUED SEARCH FOR ANSWERS

During my research it became very clear that I did, in fact, have an extreme case of bipolar. It was a strange experience to feel as if I was perfectly normal, yet know, deep down, that something was terribly wrong. Researching bipolar and all its medications and treatments helped, as it made facing my mental disorder less personal. The more I read the more committed I became to my medications and even my therapy.

Wanting and trying to get better became increasingly infuriating over the next two months. The harder I tried to control my swings with therapy, group support and medications, the more it felt that I wasn't getting better, nor could get better. Not only was my bipolar continuing to control my life, but when my mania wasn't sharpening my mind and speeding the world and reality around me, I felt sluggish, dim and stupid. The side effects of my daily medications were also getting worse. Countless times I would walk upstairs and into the kitchen only to stand motionless, wondering why I had come to the kitchen in the first place. My balance and vision were also affected, and I began to trip and walk into walls. I even fell down the stairs once, crashing through the drywall and cracking two wooden studs with my weight and momentum. However, what concerned my family more than the side effects was that my physical health was also beginning to deteriorate.

After moving down from the mountains to Denver, I had found a great doctor who I trusted completely. When Dr. Smith wasn't monitoring my blood levels, Dr. Simon took care of me. Not only was Dr. Simon one of the smartest doctors I had ever worked with, he was utterly devoted to his work. I was lucky to have him and more importantly, I felt like I could confide in him. My stomach problems, which I had struggled with my entire life, became bad enough that I always immediately located an available bathroom when walking into a building. My mother decided that was the final straw and made an appointment for me to see Dr. Simon.

Nearly five weeks after my incident in Estes Park, my mania had finally peaked and, like clockwork, it was followed by a crash into another depression. I was in my twenties and I still wasn't able to get to the doctor by myself. When I was manic, I avoided doctors because I didn't feel like I needed them or no one could find me, while during my depressions, I just didn't want to move. Because I was having some health issues and was unable to do anything on my own, my amazing mother drove me to Dr. Simon's office.

My mother motioned for me to take a seat in the waiting room while she signed me in. I plopped down in the corner, trying to keep as much distance from everyone as I could. Everyone's voices seemed loud and I ached all over, wanting nothing more than to be home, escaping the world around me with the aid of sleep.

"Kirk Miller," called a kind nurse named Suzie. Some of the staff were a bit cold to me, but I was hardly a charmer when depressed. Standing up took more effort than I had expected, but eventually I was on my feet and inching forward. Suzie saw me and opened the door to the hallway filled with examination rooms, pointing to the last room. "You're at the end Kirk," Suzie said gently, quickly seeing that I wasn't feeling well. I didn't want to be at the doctor's, but I was tired of my gut and stomach always aching. Going to the bathroom more than ten times a day was also getting tiring.

"Here," my mother's voice was calm and gentle as she came over to help me. Although I was depressed, I was still irritable in my early stages, so when my mother reached out to take hold of my arm and help me, I shook it away, speaking back in a harsh tone.

"I'm moving as fast as I can. Just give me a break." Everyone in the waiting room was judging me for the way I had lashed out at my mother, but I didn't care. Suzie was well aware that I had more than simple health problems and was used to seeing me in a foul mood. She never held it against me.

Suzie dutifully escorted us back to the exam room with professional courtesy. After closing the door behind us and waiting for me to sit up on the exam table covered with a light pink fabric and paper that crackled when I sat down, Suzie pulled out her pen and began asking questions. "Are you at the same weight?" When I nodded, she continued. "What medications are you taking?"

It is hard to look at the past, knowing that I wasn't even aware of how much of each medication I was taking. I was also oblivious to the dosage. Had I been living on my own like most men in their early twenties, I think staying on my medications would have been more difficult. Maybe impossible. I'm also very aware that the burden I caused my family was a heavy one. As I stared blankly at Suzie, my mother answered for me. "He's taking the same dosage of Lithium, clonazepam, Lamictal and Synthroid. Same as our last visit."

"What about the other medications?"

"Dr. Smith took him off the anti-psychotic since it didn't seem to be helping but hasn't changed anything since."

"Okay then," Suzie stated after she finished writing down the booklet of medications I was taking. She then took my temperature and blood pressure with the same unflappable calm as ever. Dr. Simon's staff was always top notch, most of them quick thinkers able to multitask, and many of them preparing for medical school. After removing the thermometer, Suzie returned to her clipboard, asking, "So why are we seeing you today?"

"I'm having some stomach issues."

Before Suzie could ask me what kind of issues, I followed up my statement with: "I'd prefer to talk about it with Dr. Simon." It wasn't that I was embarrassed, but I felt more comfortable talking about my bowel movements to a guy. It was bad enough that my family had noticed my problem.

"Okay then," Suzie slid my file into the wooden slot resting on the front of the door and paused before leaving. "Dr. Simon will be with you in a jiffy."

When Suzie closed the door, I laid down on the exam table. My legs were hanging off and I wasn't even lying down straight, but I didn't care. I closed my eyes and tried to find some measure of relief. When the door opened, I sat up slowly. My mother greeted Dr. Simon with a hug and smile. Dr. Simon had a closed practice and for a good reason. He was one of a kind when it came to doctors.

Since Dr. Simon had delivered me and my sister and had known my mother for a long time, he had made room for us. I didn't go to him because we had history, I went to him, as did my family, because he was the best doctor we had ever dealt with. Had he been aware of the problems I would cause, he still would've accepted us with open arms. He was simply a great guy and a once-in-a-lifetime doctor.

An older man with gray hair, Dr. Simon was always dressed in a suit and red tie. The outfit was topped off by the expensive stethoscope that always hung around his neck. He had grown up in the days before people understood how dangerous smoking was, so his voice, although warm and gentle, had a bit of a rasp to it as he greeted my mother. "Hi, Jeanne," he said warmly before turning to face me. He took one look at me and stated, "You don't look so good." Looking down at the chart, he quickly looked at all my numbers before asking. "So what's the problem with your stomach?"

"I'm going to the bathroom a lot."

"What do you mean by 'a lot'?" Dr. Simon asked. "A number or a guess would help me out."

Although I was trying to eat healthy, I wasn't lying when I told him, "Over ten times per day."

My mother interjected, "Simon, every time we go somewhere, the first thing he looks for is a bathroom and some days it is far more than ten times."

Dr. Simon just nodded. "Well, I'd say that's more trips than a young one like yourself should be making. Can you lie back?" I did as I was told as Dr. Simon came and pressed on my stomach, making small circles with his fingertips. As he was examining me, he turned to my mother and asked, "What have you tried?" Dr. Simon knew that my father was a pharmacist and was smart enough to assume that we had tried as much as we could before visiting him.

My mother listed off vitamins and probiotics and then a few medications that made Dr. Simon's smile begin to fade. Although he was an older man, his eyes were sharp and you could almost see the man thinking as my mother added, "We've tried everything, but nothing seems to help."

Dr. Simon stopped pressing on my stomach and stepped back. "You can sit up," he said, waiting for me before asking, "What do your stools look like?" Dr. Simon had a way of making even the most embarrassing questions seem harmless, so I answered.

"I usually have diarrhea." After I answered a few more questions, explaining the constant pain and urgency to go to the bathroom, Dr. Simon appeared to have made up his mind.

"I think it would be wise to schedule a colonoscopy, but in the meantime, I'm going to prescribe Prednisone." Seeing my mom's eyes widen at the mention of the drug, I was curious.

Although I didn't feel like a conversation, I did want to know. "And what is Prednisone?"

"It's a powerful steroid that is commonly used to treat inflammation. I'm only giving you a small dose for a few days, so keep a close eye on your improvement."

"Steroid?" I wondered why any doctor would prescribe such a thing. I had heard nothing good about steroids and the media made steroids seem worse than many of the hardcore drugs I had used on the street.

Dr. Simon smiled, knowing exactly what I was thinking. "Prednisone is a corticosteroid, not an anabolic steroid like you hear about athletes using in sports. I think you have Irritable Bowel Syndrome and although Prednisone isn't my first choice, it sounds like your dad has already tried all my preferred options. Your problem is severe enough that we'll give Prednisone a chance and see how you do. You only have enough for five days, so we'll re-evaluate in a week." With that, Dr. Simon wrote me a prescription and said goodbye to my mother before he stepped out of the room.

"And yet another pill." I had spoken quietly, but my mother caught my words. She walked over and gave me a hug. I could feel the concern transmitted through her embrace. I stared down at the prescription and said exactly what I was thinking. "I'm tired of this, mom."

And yet my middle-aged mother had enough endurance for the both of us.

"I know you are, sweetie. Let's go." With that, we walked out of the exam room and drove directly to the pharmacy. e We sat and waited for the pharmacist to fill the Prednisone prescription. Just sitting in the car, my gut and stomach were churning. The only way I could lessen my pain was to lean forward and clutch my stomach. My stomach ached badly enough that I was actually looking forward to taking the medication that Dr. Simon had prescribed. It was beyond my ability to feel optimistic; my life, and now my body, were falling apart. I loved lifting weights and playing basketball when

I wasn't depressed, but lately the combination of my depression and my stomach pain had left me sidelined.

When the pharmacist handed us the prescription, my mother opened the bag and the bottle before handing me a single pill. As Dr. Simon had instructed, I took the pill from my mother's hand and plopped it into my mouth. I had become so used to taking pills that I no longer needed water.

As I would find out, life and fate were not without a sense of humor. If I had known what taking the Prednisone would cause I would never have swallowed the pill in the first place. Prednisone was another step downwards on a long and harrowing journey directly toward using myself as a guinea pig.

***

When I awoke the next morning, my stomach still ached, but it wasn't as bad as it usually was. My depression, however, had grown more severe and had done so more quickly than in the past. Although my stomach was feeling a bit better, otherwise I felt horrible. All I wanted was to stay in bed and sleep. Only my thirst and need to relieve my bladder were enough to get me moving.

I sat up in bed for a long moment, my head hung low. Even as small slits of sun came in through my window, everything felt dark to me. The colors of the posters on my wall looked dim again and I had no idea how I would face another day.

I sighed, a deep and lengthy one that failed to clear any of the thick awful feelings congealing within. I reached up to rub my eyes because they itched, but the moment my hands touched my face, I paused. Something wasn't right. I ran my fingers slowly, very gently over my face, and felt small bumps covering my skin. Unlike zits, these bumps were softer and broke when touched. I had had it with aggravating side effects of medications. As if the dizziness, the hair loss, the trembling, the confusion, and the leaden emotionlessness weren't enough, now some new issue? I cursed and forced myself up onto my feet, then headed towards the bathroom in a frustrated daze. I should've felt a sense of panic, but the bleakness of my world view overpowered my normal thought process.

I flicked on the lights in my small basement bathroom and peered into the mirror. Covering my entire body were small bumps that looked like sunburn blisters. Each blister was filled with a clear liquid and certainly wasn't a zit. I had seen them before on my face, but only one or two. "Son of a..." I said quietly, wanting to curse but not having the energy.

I touched one. The blister was so soft that it broke open, releasing a clear liquid. I remember shrugging and deciding that I must have had some allergic reaction that sleep would cure. As soon as I turned away from the mirror, planning on returning to my bedroom, I noticed my mother standing in the doorway holding a food tray piled with breakfast. When she saw the blisters covering my body her eyes widened and she nearly dropped the tray.

She set down the food and rushed to my side. "What happened?" she asked, her shock quieting her voice as it came out more like a whisper. Her tone quickly changed as she turned away from me and shouted loudly enough that it made me cringe. "Jackson!"

My father must've heard the panic in my mother's voice, because I heard my dad's feet running down the stairs above me. It was Friday and my dad had just happened to have the day off.

"Mom, it's not a big deal. Just let me go back to bed." I tried to move past her, but she held her ground and I didn't have the energy to argue, so I backed up and leaned against the edge of my sink.

Rushing down the stairs so fast that he nearly tripped over the breakfast tray on the stairs, my dad ran into the bathroom with wide eyes. My mom's shout had startled him, to say the least. "What's wrong?" Seeing that there was no major emergency, my father took a breath of relief, even with my mom pointing at my face like I was mostly dead already.

When it came to medical issues, my father never panicked. To me, my father had always seemed more like a doctor than a pharmacist, always knowing what we had before it was confirmed by a test or a doctor. I had always respected his medical opinions, so I just sighed and let him come close enough to take a look. "Looks like sunburn blisters," he mumbled to himself before stepping back and adding, "Are the blisters anywhere else?"

"I just woke up. How would I know?"

"Kirk Patrick!" My mother always used my middle name when she was upset or with me. "Please don't talk to your father like that." The truth was that as much as I respected and loved my father, I never spoke to him with respect. I was usually very short and impatient with him without any good reason.

"Fine," I retorted as I stripped off my shirt. "Are you both happy now?" When I saw my mother's face turn pale and my father's eyes shimmer with surprise, I looked down. The blisters were not only on my face. In fact, they ran down my arms, chest, back, stomach and even my legs. "What the…" I began, but my mom was in full panic mode now.

She interrupted me. "Dr. Simon is out of the office today, Jackson. What should we do?" My mother was beyond worried. Indeed, she was on the verge of tears and pleading with my father for answers.

As always, my dad remained calm. "There is no reason to panic. This isn't a reaction that I'm familiar with, but Simon won't know. We need to get into a dermatologist."

"Another freakin' doctor." I threw up my hands up. "Wouldn't it be easier if someone just shot me?" I didn't realize at the time how dark my statement was, but it was the final straw, causing my mother's eyes to tear and concern to fill my father's.

My mother was out of the bathroom like a flash.. She was on the phone with Bonnie moments later. I knew she had called Dr. Simon's office to get advice, and as my mother talked in the basement's main room, my father continued to inspect my blisters. Without looking away from the blisters, he spoke quietly. "You shouldn't talk like that. It upsets your mother and to be frank, I don't like it either." I would have responded, but my father asked me a question before I was able to. "Did you eat anything different yesterday?"

"No, but I did start taking Prednisone."

My father shook his head.

Meanwhile my mother was in the midst of raising her voice, shouting that she didn't care what their rules were.

"That's strange. If anything I would expect that the Prednisone would have helped the blisters. It certainly wouldn't cause them." Reaching up, he touched my face where I had popped one of the blisters. "Now that is odd." When he pulled back his hand, he held his finger up to the light so that I could see. The liquid that had come out of my blister had dried, turning into what looked like an amber crystal. "Looks like dermatitis herpetiformis, but does it itch?"

"No." My response caused my dad to pause and reflect.

"It isn't related to the Lamictal, but I still don't like it."

I might have found humor in how complex my body was if I wasn't so despondent. I put my shirt back on, and felt the slimy, but not painful sensation of several more blisters popping from the fabric sliding across. My dad was not the type to worry, but when he had left the bathroom, I had caught just a flash of concern in his eyes. All I knew is that there was no way I would be getting into any dermatologist that day. Most appointments were weeks out, which I knew because I had suffered from bad acne when I was younger. I was already heading out of the bathroom and towards my bedroom when I felt my mother take hold of my wrist.

"Get dressed, we have an appointment in thirty minutes."

III. THE IMPULSIVE ANSWER

I had not expected my mom to be able to get an appointment, especially on the same day that she called, but when push came to shove she could move mountains. After giving me my daily handful of pills, we got into the car and my mom took off, driving fast enough that our thirty-minute drive only took twenty.

She headed into the building indestructible and ready. She pointed to the waiting area before stalking toward the reception window. "You just go sit down and relax; I'll fill everything out."

I nodded and meandered over to a large fish tank in the center of the waiting room. Fish of all colors and patterns darted through the fake coral and plants in the tank. Years later I'd look back and wonder how I never noticed how brilliant the colors were. Although the fish did nothing to cheer me up, they were better than sitting in the waiting room with a bunch of strangers.

I waited there, bored and tired even after sleeping for over ten hours. I didn't even hear my mother shouting at the nurses that she didn't care if we had to wait all day. Unaware of anything but the darkness that was holding me prisoner, I slid down the chair and rested my head on the back cushion. Just as I was about to close my eyes, a nurse called my name. I would learn years later that the only reason they had agreed to see me was because my mother had caused such a stir. There is no force as strong as a protective and loving mother. That I now take as simple fact.

After a nurse showed me to a large and high-tech exam room with bright paintings and light that hurt my eyes, she quickly took down my medical history before pressing a small red button on the wall. She addressed my distraught mother with that same cool professionalism. "Dr. Wright will be with you in a moment."

"Dr. Simon told me that Dr. Wright was the best dermatologist he knew," my mother explained, adding, "I'm sure it's nothing, but if your dad thinks you should have your skin looked at, well, you know how he is." My dad was really laid back, so if he was worried we all took the situation seriously.

Dr. Wright walked in only a few moments later. At first he seemed a bit annoyed as we had forced our way into an appointment. That quickly changed when he saw my face and neck. He shut the door silently and got right to business.

Dr. Wright was a tall man in a neatly pressed lab coat that matched the white hair that lined the sides of his bald head. His thick square glasses made his eyes look comically large, but he was all about business. Without a word, he sat down on his stool and examined my blisters with gloved hands. Rolling back and pressing on the intercom, Dr. Wright's voice was sharp and commanding. "I need surgical equipment for a biopsy in exam room six."

"So you're going to cut out a blister?" I asked. "I've had blisters like this before, just never so many." I didn't care about the biopsy, but I just wasn't in the mood for anything that day and getting a piece of my skin cut out was not exactly on my top ten list of fun things to do.

"I need to take two, actually. If you could take off your shirt, please," Dr. Wright said. Moments later a nurse appeared with a tray of surgical tools. "Kirk, if you've had them before and it is worse now, I'd like to know what I'm dealing with, so I'm going to take two biopsies, one to send to a university and one to our lab. If your condition is getting worse, especially after taking prednisone, then we need to make sure we know what is going on so that we treat it properly."

It was a good answer and I didn't have the energy to argue, so I took off my shirt and laid back on the table as Dr. Wright took two biopsies from the center of my chest while setting up an appointment for the following week. After he stitched up one of the larger cuts and left the room, I put my shirt on and sighed. "Can we go home?"

I don't know how I must have sounded, but my mother's face fell. "Of course, sweetie."

One week later, I was back in the same examination room, totally unaware of the bad news I was about to receive.

***

Most of my blisters had faded away, but many still remained. Since my depression had moved into its second stage I was having extremely dark thoughts. It wasn't possible to go out in public due to my blisters, and this only made me hate everything with a higher intensity. With my mind feeling dark and slow, it took both my sister and mother to get me out of bed, dressed and into the car so that I could make my appointment with Dr. Wright.

Once at the doctor's office, my sister came to the passenger side door, opened it and reached out to take hold of my hand. "Kirken," as my family often called me, "let's get you into that office so you can enjoy the rest of the day." As always, my sister was trying her hardest to smile and help keep my mother from breaking down into tears. What I owe my family, I can never repay, which is one reason why I am writing about my life. I owe much of my full recovery to the support of my family and close friends.

When my sister got me out of the car, I held onto her tiny frame. I didn't feel up to the task of walking into the doctor's office and eventually the exam room. I was still taking the prednisone along with all my other medications as Dr. Wright, Dr. Simon and my father all figured it would help, but I was getting only minute relief from my stomach problems and now my skin had caused a new problem. As I sat in the exam room, I truly believed that my family would be better off without me. The suicidal thoughts had become common over the last few days and not knowing what was wrong with my skin had only made me feel that much more useless. Luckily, although I had every intention of ending my own life, by the time I wanted to, I was too depressed and tired to act. Had I been just a bit happier or energized, or even on an antidepressant, I know I would have taken my life during the second stage of my depressions.

My sister understood my situation deeply, and sat next to me on the exam table, patting my back while we waited to hear what the results of my tests were. Dr. Wright entered some time later in the same quiet, intense way as before, but this time took the time to introduce himself to us all before examining my blisters once more. "The tests came back and you have what is referred to as Linear IgA dermatosis. It is an incredibly rare autoimmune disease that causes blistering just beneath the skin. Had we not sent it to the university, I doubt we would have figured it out so quickly. I thought it might have been dermatitis herpetiformis, but it didn't present in the same ways."

I had been researching enough medical journals and studies that I knew exactly what an autoimmune disease was. To say that it was bad news was an understatement. Not only was my mind a mess, but my own immune system was attacking itself.

"So what's the treatment?" My sister asked. I already figured I'd need more pills and I wasn't wrong.

"Well," Dr. Wright paused and took a deep breath before continuing. "Usually, we would give a corticosteroid to control your current outburst, but it isn't a good long-term treatment and you're already taking prednisone which should have suppressed your blisters in the first place. The long-term solution that I would suggest is taking a drug called Dapsone."

Dr. Wright explained that I would need to have regular blood tests so that they could make sure the Dapsone wasn't causing major damage, especially with my combination of other drugs. I would've laughed at the idea of being on another medication that had the potential to kill me had I been able. The appointment flew by and before I knew it I was back home and my mother had added yet another drug to my long list of medications. I was at the point now where I had to take my pills separated into three times per day and multiple swallows just because there were too many.

Luckily, after taking the Dapsone my blisters cleared right up. When I saw Dr. Simon and he heard about what had happened with the prednisone, he was as stumped as Dr. Wright had been. He was not happy about pulling me off the prednisone which had finally begun to help my stomach, but had not liked the reaction it had caused.

***

Two weeks later, even though my stomach pains and bathroom trips returned to normal, I was finally climbing out of my depression. After taking a long shower, shaving and eating a small breakfast, I was in the mood to continue with my research. When I walked upstairs and into the kitchen to take my pills I wasn't sure why my sister and mother seemed on edge. Whenever I cleaned myself up, it was a sign to my mother and sister that the worst of my downs were gone. I wouldn't learn this until years later, nor did I know that they both couldn't help wondering when my mania would overtake me and if I would simply vanish one day. Their fears were very justified.

I took my pills and headed down to my room with a bottle of water, ready to spend the day researching. I sat down in my chair and turned on my computer, then with typical ramping mania energy, cleared my desk of all the loose medical journals and research articles. The moment I sat down my stomach tightened up and I bent over to lessen the pain. Dr. Simon had been quite displeased with my reaction to prednisone, acknowledging that although the prednisone had cut my pain and my IBS to a manageable level, the risks of continuing to take the medication were beyond his comfort level. At the moment, I thought the blisters were worth it. I had been given a short taste of what it was like to live without debilitating pain, making it all the more obvious now.

Frustrated at my options, I was convinced that if I couldn't take prednisone or any other corticosteroid, there had to be something else that would act similarly to prednisone. I was in enough pain that I set aside my research on bipolar and started looking into something that might help my stomach.

After a few days of researching something that wasn't a corticosteroid but had similar anti-inflammatory benefits, I found an interesting study comparing the ability of cortisone and something called nandrolone decanoate. The research being done had analyzed and compared the two drugs, evaluating which was more beneficial in controlling inflammation and healing torn muscles in three groups of rats. Although the nandrolone decanoate was not as effective as the cortisone when it came to reducing inflammation, the drug still gave far better results than the control group. Also, the rats that were given nandrolone decanoate had surpassed the control and cortisone groups in overall health by such a wide margin. I was stunned and fascinated.

Hence, I began my research into nandrolone decanoate. When I began my side research I had no idea that nandrolone was an anabolic steroid or that its use was illegal without a written prescription. After a day of reading, I was amazed that the drug wasn't used more often. Not only did it have some anti-inflammatory benefits, but it has been shown to be incredibly helpful with many major diseases and injuries. Due to the stigma of anabolic steroids, however, it was never talked about and I knew no doctor would prescribe it for Irritable Bowel Syndrome.

Had I been a sane individual and traditionally trained in medicine I would have discounted the use of nandrolone decanoate due to its legality. It did have side effects, but they were seen mostly on women and men taking higher than therapeutic doses. I wasn't sane and was certainly not shy about risks. After a bit more research, I decided I was going to take control of my own body. To say the least, this was my mania speaking and was a terrible idea, but I didn't live in everyone else's world. I lived in my own, making my own rules and the ability to break them easy.

Over the next few months, I continued to learn more about the compound nandrolone decanoate. Multiple studies from prestigious universities had used the drug to help patients with everything from AIDS to arthritis and Lupus. As my mania kicked up, I acted, unaware that my life would forever be changed.

IV. DIVING HEADFIRST INTO SELF-EXPERIMENTATION

The more I researched all the medical uses for anabolic steroids, the more astonished I grew that the use of such drugs was looked down upon by almost all medical professionals. I was aware that some individuals interested in increasing their athletic performance would abuse such drugs, but I couldn't fathom why the drug itself was not being applied more often in normal medical situations. Needless to say, it became all too clear that there wasn't a doctor on the planet that would write me a prescription for such a drug. As I continued to suffer from the pain my IBS caused me as well as more consistent problems with my skin, I did what I had always done when I wanted something but couldn't have it. I went around the law to procure what I desired.

Since I had more than enough connections in the illicit drug market, I made some calls and set up a meeting. The main problem with getting hold of nandrolone decanoate was that it was commonly counterfeited. Although none of my sources for drugs dealt anything like anabolic steroids, eventually I landed a solid connection.

After sending several coded messages by email, I was told how much money to send with explicit instructions on where and how to send the cash. A normal individual would've thought twice about sending cash in the mail, but I was told my source was not only the best, but well known in steroid and athletic circles. To him, my order was small, but because he knew a mutual friend, he decided to work with me.

I followed this new source's instructions closely, and a package showed up at my house two weeks later. Thinking back, I can't believe I wasn't worried about someone finding my incoming package and opening it. Although my mother didn't open my mail, she did, on occasion, open something up by mistake. I did not want to explain what I had ordered, especially to my dad who knew, as well as I, that even possessing anabolic steroids without a prescription was treated swiftly and severely. I was solidly in the early stages of mania and unable to see beyond my current needs, or the present. I never even thought about the ramifications for getting caught.

Home alone when the package was dropped off, I was excited to see what I had paid a few hundred dollars for. I handled it like a bomb, relayed it gingerly to the bathroom, shut the door, and opened the package. It was time to be a guinea pig.

***

I counted twenty small boxes containing 2 ml vials of nandrolone decanoate in the small package. The boxes were taped and packaged to avoid any damage during their shipment. It took some time to extract each of the tiny vial-filled boxes and inspect everything for damage, but once that was done, I returned to the box and retrieved the remainder of my order. Since I had been manic at the time I had placed my order, I had also ordered twenty glass ampoules of Testosterone Enanathate that looked filled with a light yellow baby oil. Lastly, I retrieved the twenty syringes I had ordered along with the medications. I knew where and how to inject the nandrolone decanoate, but I had expected small needles like the ones I had used for illicit drugs. Instead, these needles were over an inch long, which should've made me nervous, but before I even considered that I might be making a mistake, I loaded a syringe, poked the long needle through my skin where I was supposed to and pushed the oily substance into my body. It never occurred to me that I could've died had the vials been filled with some unknown substance or bacteria. To me, it was time to take action and fix my body. I was tired of the doctors trying and, being in my second stage of mania, thought I knew better. The truth was that I was a fool.

After removing the needle, I sat down and stared at the illegal drugs sitting on my desk with a thin and dangerous smile playing across my lips. I had researched the proper dosages as well as how to properly administer the injectable esters, but that didn't change the fact that I was playing a hunch, hoping the anabolic would help my IBS as the prednisone had, or had begun to, before the skin condition took effect. With no way of knowing and no instant feeling from the injection, I shrugged and cleaned the droplet of blood from the injection site. Only looking back do I see the risks I was taking. Not only did I have enough of the substance to be held as a distributor, punishable as a federal crime, but I didn't even know if the stuff was real.

Looking at the empty vial I smiled. I had done my research, taken the plunge both literally and figuratively, and knew it was now simply a waiting game.

Three days later, my stomach hadn't improved, and my mania was growing in intensity. I had carefully hidden all my drugs and syringes so that no one would discover them, but I was growing impatient. I was supposed to be feeling better, but I wasn't. The studies I had carefully read and researched had shown nandrolone decanoate to work as an anti-inflammatory, all while strengthening my bones and my immune system, so I wasn't pleased that nothing had improved. Well into my second stage of my mania, I was angry that I wasn't making any progress, figuring that if one vial didn't work, perhaps I needed more. That day I did three more injections, making my weekly dose of nandrolone more than four times the medical dose for males. Even knowing that it took time for the anabolic steroids to enter and affect my system, I wasn't thinking straight and as usual my logic and knowledge could not compete with the power of my mania.

As the next few days went on, my skin blistered violently, and I had to double my dose of Dapsone to keep the blisters and itching under control. I was supposed to do one injection a week and it had already been five days, making me wonder if I should inject more. I had spent some time at the gym and hadn't noticed a difference in strength either, making me wonder if my contact had ripped me off. Angry and frustrated, I went through every possible way, in my mind, that I might get my money back for the drugs that had to be fake. After a few hours of tossing and turning while thinking of revenge, I fell asleep.

The next day when I awoke to the sound of my alarm, I reached up to rub my eyes but stopped when I realized that my stomach, usually aching and churning after a night's sleep, was calm and painless. The sudden realization of what happened struck me, and I laughed out loud. I lay in bed and ran my hands over my stomach before hitting the bed with both hands in celebration. Although I needed to release my bladder, I felt no pain and no urgency to go to the bathroom for the first time in months. On top of not having any pain, the extra dose of Dapsone must have helped because my skin was clear of all blisters.

"So he did send me the real stuff," I said with a smile, and rolled out of bed. I would quickly discover that my contact had indeed sent me the real thing. The true effects of my self-experimentation would take some time to reveal themselves.

***

That day, I decided I'd give my stomach a test, eating some fried food and candy that usually made my stomach worse. "Kirk," my mother said, seeing what I was about to eat. "You shouldn't eat that, or it will upset your stomach."

"Not today," I said with a grin that made my mother's face fill with concern.

Not knowing what to expect, she touched my shoulder and added, "Just go slow, okay."

I nodded. It was important to see if this was just a fluke or if I had been right. With mania on the menu, I'd already decided that if the medication worked, I would be ordering more. Besides ordering more, I also knew that I wasn't going to start with 200 milligrams. If the dose I was taking worked, I wasn't about to change it. Not only was I foolish, but anyone who has studied androgenic anabolic steroids would tell me that I was taking far more than was medically necessary. Had I been aware of myself, my mania or my actions I might have thought twice about trying a lower dose, if for no other reason than cost. At my current dose, I would be out of the nandrolone in four weeks and without a job, my credit cards would only provide me with so many cash withdrawals. None of it mattered at that moment though. I was overjoyed that my stomach was free of pain and all because I tried something other doctors hadn't and wouldn't. My vision of myself was certainly grandiose, making me believe even more that I could find something to cure my bipolar too. When my stomach stayed steady and calm even with all the food I had thrown at it, I began to widen my research to both bipolar and anabolic steroids.

For two weeks, my mania stayed steady, allowing me to gather a massive amount of information about anabolic steroids and bipolar. Most individuals that used the drugs recreationally would do what they called a 'cycle', staying on the steroids for a certain amount of time before giving their body a rest. Anabolic steroids did have side effects, which were important to look into more deeply, not because I was worried, but because of how many men and women reported having symptoms much like bipolar when coming on and off their cycles. To be fair, many of the individuals in these articles were grossly abusing the anabolic steroids, but still, something seemed to click as I researched. Regardless of the side effects, my stomach had completely normalized, and my skin blisters had vanished, so I wasn't about to stop taking the drugs.

As I began to gain size and strength while weight training, my body weight also began to increase at a more dramatic rate than normal. No one in my family would consider that I was taking anabolic steroids, so they just thought I was working out more consistently. Although my physical health was improving, my bipolar was still present and I continued to have swings of both depressions and mania, yet I was feeling just a slight bit more stable. It certainly wasn't an amazing difference, but something had changed.

After six months of taking the anabolic steroids, I could sometimes see my moods, only now it wasn't just for a brief moment. My family had noticed that my swings were happening less often, and I had started teaching the violin again, this time without canceling every other time. I only had two students at the time, but I had never been able to handle one. Although I was still having swings, I began to realize that something was happening. I had been taking my bipolar drugs for over five years, but they had never made me as stable as I currently was. Therefore, I began to wonder if, against all odds and medical science, the anabolic steroids were helping me. I never told anyone what I was taking, but it was only a matter of time before I would have to tell Dr. Simon.

***

Nicoal had finished her associate's degree and moved to Colorado to finish her business degree. Luckily, at the beginning of our real relationship,

I tended to be more manic than depressed, but eventually I had no choice but to tell her that I was bipolar before getting married. I had been fearing the conversation, but when I told her, she simply shook her head and said something I will never forget: "No, you don't." Her denial was proof that love truly was blind as I was not easy to handle, nor would most women be strong enough to handle me when I couldn't handle myself.

The longer we lived together in my parent's basement, the more my actions became too wild and explosive, making the truth apparent to her. In the face of my confession and the evidence, she decided to give our marriage a chance. She then also agreed to stay with me and wait for me to beat the bipolar. Knowing who she is now, I know that our relationship would never have lasted, especially if she had ever learned about the anabolic steroids. Luckily for me, she stayed around long enough to see me improve, even if at a very slow pace.

I had gained around twenty-five pounds since I began injecting myself with anabolic steroids, not all of it muscle as the media would have people believe. I'm not saying that the anabolic steroids didn't help me gain weight, but I wasn't working out consistently enough to utilize the large doses I was taking. However, because the steroids had calmed my IBS, it was the first time in my life I had found it easy to keep food inside me, and that naturally led to me gaining weight. Unfortunately, I never thought that my large physique would raise some red flags when it was time for my annual physical. I was blinded by the elation of my first ever bout of success, and who could blame me?

While Nicoal was taking classes, my mother had scheduled an appointment with Dr. Simon as it was the only time she could go, and I still wasn't at the point where I could really take care of myself. Unlike our usual visits to the doctor I was in a good mood that day, joking with my mom as we drove down to Dr. Simon's office. Our family had been doing better, although my last manic peak had ended with me smashing every piece of scrap wood we had in our garage, not stopping even after my hands were bloody. It was the first time since Estes Park that Nicoal had seen my animalistic rage. Although my actions were similar to past manic explosions, my family later told me that they were surprised. Not because I was lashing out with violence, but because it appeared that I was selecting what I broke, as if deep down, I was thinking of the value of what I was destroying. Although I hate the memory, it was perhaps the first time others saw that something was different about my swings.

96

Once more, my mother signed me in. I took a seat, flipping through a magazine without really paying attention. Honestly, I had become used to the doctor's visits by now, but by this time I was ready to stop. I was on my way out of this, and more, I'd done it without the help of the so-called experts. Although I still had swings, everyone felt like I was far better than ever before. I waved my mother over and gestured to the seat next to mine.

"Mom, you should read this article." I had no idea that even the way I was treating my mother was different. She regarded me warily, but eventually got up and took a seat next to me.

After about twenty minutes, Suzie called my name. I had expected her to lead me to the same exam room we always had, but she stopped me and pointed to the scale, saying, "You've certainly bulked up since I last saw you."

"Lots of protein and working out." I stepped up onto the scale. Since I didn't always have to go to the bathroom, I had been able to keep some weight on and my strength had certainly improved, but no matter what anyone thinks, anabolic steroids don't make an athlete, hard work does, but that is another issue entirely.

Suzie had to adjust the scale. Her face registered surprise when the scale came to a balance. "So how much have I gained?" I asked after the scale came to a balance.

"Thirty-six pounds," Suzie said, her voice a mix of worry and surprise. "That's quite a bit of weight to pack on in eight months."

My mother smiled and said, "He's been at the gym more consistently and his IBS is gone." It was obvious that she was pleased that I was staying more stable, yet she had no idea that I was taking anything other than my bipolar medications, nor did anyone else.

Suzie led us to the last room, checking my temperature and asking her standard questions while she took my blood pressure. "Your blood pressure is high, but everything else seems fine. Dr. Simon will be with you in a moment."

Dr. Simon entered the room wearing a sleek blue blazer and skinny red tie. He gave my mother a quick hug before turning towards me. When he saw me, his eyes sharpened, and he looked down at the chart. "So how has your IBS been?"

"I've been doing really well," I responded, not sure how to explain that I had gone from having chronic pain and constant diarrhea to having a regular schedule. "No complaints here."

Dr. Simon looked at my mother and smiled. "Would you mind stepping out? I have to check a few things." My mother quickly nodded and left the room. When the door closed, Dr. Simon sat down next to me. I noted the intense stare and the firm tone. "Now that your mom's gone, why don't you tell me what's really going on. Your IBS is gone, you've gained more weight than is normal. I've been doing this for a while, you know."

I was a bit startled at the severity of Dr. Simon's voice, but what really caught me off guard was the question itself. I certainly didn't want to tell the only doctor I trusted that I was taking anabolic steroids, but I figured that Dr. Simon would figure it out eventually. So I told him everything, from how I thought up the idea to how it had gotten rid of my IBS. I even expressed that my skin hadn't blistered for nearly three months now. To my own surprise, I also mentioned that since starting the steroids, I was feeling more stable. Never before had I ever mentioned stability to anyone. Hell, I'd never been able to gauge myself now.

Dr. Simon met my eyes with a cold stare filled with disappointment, a touch of anger and also fascination. When he spoke, his voice was cold, and his words chosen carefully. "You have put me in a horrible position, Kirk. I can't support your use of anabolic steroids. And at the dosage you are taking, are you even aware of the side effects?" He sighed and he shook his head. "I certainly can't write you a prescription."

"I know you can't," I blurted, sensing that he was growing more upset the longer he thought about what I had done, "and I would never ask you to, but the truth is that I've never felt better. As for the drugs, I can get them myself and won't ever ask you for a prescription. My source is good and the only reason I didn't tell you, or anyone for that matter, was because I knew no one would approve, but the results..."

This time, Dr. Simon cut me off. Although he looked angry, I could see a glimmer of curiosity in his eyes. "So you haven't told anyone?" When I nodded, he continued. "I should drop you as a patient, but it's my job to help. Although I can't support what you're doing, I can't stop you. Since I can't control you I have a responsibility to make sure you are safe." Simon leaned back in his chair, his hands resting on his small belly. "Are you willing to do bi-weekly blood tests, keep track of your IBS, linear IGA and mood swings?"

"Yes," I said quickly. I sensed that although he didn't agree with what I was doing, he wasn't about to let me kill myself on his watch.

"If you slip up or do anything without consulting me..."

"I won't. You have my word."

Dr. Simon nodded, adding, "Then I'll try my best to keep you safe." He opened the door and asked Suzie to get my mother. We sat quietly for a moment as we waited. I knew that Dr. Simon couldn't tell anyone what we had just discussed, so I was a bit curious as to why he had wanted to see my mother. When she entered, he wasted no time as he asked: "So, Jeanne, how have Kirk's mood swings been? And be honest." He was checking my story, which I just thought was intelligent.

My mother locked eyes with me, no doubt wondering if she truly could be honest. I nodded and my mother actually smiled. "He's been far more stable over the past four months and he's even been able to work."

I could tell that Dr. Simon was both skeptical and worried, but he had Suzie write me up for a host of blood tests, put a smile on for my mother and gave her a quick hug. "I want to see Kirk more regularly, so have Bonnie set up an appointment for next week." After my mother said that she would, Dr. Simon turned to me. "I'll see you soon." The look he gave me felt like a reminder that I had agreed to his demands and was not to cross him. I simply nodded as he turned and left the room.

After setting up my next appointment, my mother and I left. I skimmed the page with the blood order and was astonished at how many tests Dr. Simon had ordered. He wasn't kidding about making sure I was okay, and I didn't mind. He was the first person that knew about what I was doing and over the next few years, he kept a very close eye on me. Strangely enough, our secret would eventually bring us closer together.

***

A full year had passed since I had started taking steroids and I was aware that long term use of anabolic steroids could cause problems. Eventually they did, but not anything I had expected. At first, the visits with Dr. Simon included a lecture that I should try and back off the steroids, but over time, as my IBS, skin and bipolar continued to improve, I could tell that Dr. Simon was growing more curious. However, he remained cautious and kept me busy with blood tests and mood charts.

As time went on I began to become more aware of my moods. For so long, I'd lacked even basic self-awareness. I still couldn't control the rising or falling, but just being aware of what was going on was an entirely new experience. Also, my manic or depressive episodes stayed away longer. This left me with longer uninterrupted periods of normality, or complete self-control. It was a novel experience, and an eye-opening one.

I felt better than ever, and my research continued into any reason why anabolic steroids might actually help someone with bipolar. There was hardly any data, and none when referencing mental health. However, the anti-inflammatory effects could be hypothesized to aid those suffering with bipolar. Other data, not regarding anabolic steroids, did point to possible inflammatory connections with mental health. Also, just the immune response and gut health were also thinly connected to mental struggles. It wasn't proof, but at least provided some scientific data I could use to draw a hypothesis. What I found was only hypothetical with small samples. I decided it was time to take my experiment a step further. Like many bipolar patients, I had stopped taking my medications before, but this time I called Dr. Simon to get permission.

After a long talk, he decided that my lithium level could be cut back slightly. The dosage was still in the toxic range, and Dr. Simon told me to take one of my four Lithium pills, cut it into eight pieces, taking all but the single eighth. Essentially lowering my total dosage by around three percent. He wouldn't let me lower my other drugs as he wanted to see how I did with one at a time. While I was breaking apart one of my Lithium pills, I didn't realize that my mother was standing behind me.

"What are you doing?" she asked, startling me. I quickly spun around to face her. "You know that you can't stop taking your medications."

I backed away from the table, showing my mom how many pieces I had divided the large pill into. "I'm not going to stop taking my medications, but I'm doing better, so I want to try and cut it down. I'm only lowering it by around three percent and Dr. Simon said it was okay." My mother's eyes began to tear up; I'm sure she was imagining me falling apart again. "How about I make a deal with you," I said to distract her from her very justified fears. My mother looked back and forth from the cut up pill to me, not saying anything. "Don't tell anyone that I'm cutting back my Lithium and if anyone feels like I'm getting worse or you do, I'll go back to 1800 milligrams."

"Give me your word," my mother said, knowing that if I gave my word, I would do my best to keep it. It was the one weird quirk that only vanished when at the peak of a mania or depression. I nodded.

"I give you my word, if I get worse, I'll up the dose." My mother walked over and hugged me, gripping me tightly. She didn't want me to get worse, but I could tell she wanted to believe I could get better. Later on, she confessed that her fear was I'd stop taking my medication entirely, especially if she continued to press the issue. In her way, she was trying to keep me safe. I didn't know until years later how much my decision had terrified and burdened her. I should never have asked her to keep such a large secret or given her the responsibility to try and watch me objectively. Surprising us both, however, I only continued to get better and more stable.

Although I was feeling better and more stable, I was still not cured of bipolar. My quality of life had increased immensely and the heavy fog that made my mind feel slow and dull from the medications thinned a bit each time Dr. Simon allowed me to drop my dosage by a tiny increment. Not only did I keep up with my charts and blood tests, but at least once a week I would ask my mother how she thought I was doing. As the rest of my family believed that all the therapy and medications were finally working, my mother was trying her best to stay objective in her assessments of my lowered dosages.

On the weeks when I had been even a bit off, my mother would be very blunt, and we wouldn't lower my medication that week. To her surprise, I didn't fight her and as the months passed and I continued to feel better, things were looking up. I felt smarter, less drugged and was even becoming more aware of my swings. My ability to sense my moods, however, did not give me any true control to stop them. During the months when I was lowering my medications, my swings hadn't vanished and I did have a few brushes with mania and depression, but each swing was less severe and lasted a shorter time. My mother never panicked even though I know she was always waiting for me to fall beyond control. Fortunately, I never did.

I don't remember exactly how long I had been taking the anabolic steroids, but I had cut both my Lithium and Lamictal down by nearly twelve percent and was doing very well mentally. I didn't know at the time, but my mother had talked to Dr. Simon, keeping him updated on how I was doing. I was in a particularly strange situation because my mother didn't know that I was experimenting with anabolic steroids while lowering my medications but knowing that Dr. Simon was carefully watching me made my mother feel better.

Since I was remaining more stable as time went on, I felt I had to come clean with my mother, telling her what I had been taking. At first, I remember her eyes widening with shock at the revelation that I, her only son, had been experimenting on myself. Her shock turned to anger given that I hadn't told her the entire truth. I was honest, telling her that I had kept her in the dark so that she could judge my moods without thinking about another variable.

"I'm calling Simon." She picked up the phone with anger in her eyes.

"He already knows." Her anger was replaced with surprised, and she replaced the phone. "I would've told you, but I wanted you to judge me without thinking about steroids."

For one of the first times, I saw the stress I had caused. My mother's eyes looked tired and I could feel her frustration. Her whole body was constantly taut with apprehension. It was my first memory of seeing how my actions affected others. I couldn't handle this realization. It was painful to watch her stand there speechless, full of conflicting emotions. After a few moments I walked over to her and gave her a hug. Her tears really started to come on hard now. These were not caused by sadness.. "Do you know how long it's been since you've given me a hug?" My mother asked. She refused to let go.

The truth is that I didn't. It is hard to look back and realize that whenever I was depressed or manic, I withheld affection. All my life, I had been so wrapped up with my own needs, seeing everyone for what value they could add to my life, that I had never thought about what others needed. When I wanted to get my way, I could read people, manipulating emotions and situations to gain what I wanted. Realizing that I had not even given my own mother the love she deserved still haunts me deeply.

"I'll get better," was all I could think to say.

With my mother knowing the entire truth, I felt like my life was finally going to turn around. Dr. Simon was monitoring my health, my IBS and Linear IGA were both gone, and my broken mind was slowly beginning to heal. What I wasn't expecting was that I was one of the rare people whose blood wasn't designed for heavy anabolic steroids use. The next few months nearly cost me my life.

***

When the symptoms first began, I hardly noticed them. I would feel hot and itchy over my entire body but there was no rash or blisters. The feeling would fade as soon as I lifted weights or had to go out into the cold. Things slowly grew worse and I would often feel an incredible urge to itch my back, chest, arms and legs. I told my father of my symptoms and he checked for a rash, but as I had told him my skin was clear. Usually, an intense itch was accompanied by some form of rash, so my symptoms were a bit mysterious.

I wondered if I was allergic to something. I checked all over the house, but my mother was still using the same detergent to wash my clothes and sheets and I hadn't changed to a different soap, shampoo or toothpaste, leaving me wondering what was causing me to itch. When the itch intensified, making me feel as if my skin was being pricked by thousands of red-hot needles, I began to wonder what was wrong. Not wanting to bother Dr. Simon, I tried researching my symptoms myself, but to no avail. When the burning no longer faded away and I began coughing, unable to stop, I knew I needed help. For the first time in my life I called the doctor and made my own appointment.

My cough and symptoms had worried my family and Nicoal wasn't able to sleep with me coughing throughout the night. Sometimes it would become so violent that the whites of my eyes would turn red, but not in a normal way. After two sleepless nights and two days of non-stop coughing, it was time for my doctor's appointment. I was planning on going alone, but my mother thought she should come in case Dr. Simon had any questions about my stability or medications. I actually think she was so taken aback by my willingness to do it myself that it confused her.

This time, when Dr. Simon entered the room, he looked worried. I wasn't aware of how red my face was and how high-pitched my cough had gotten. It was obvious that I wasn't suffering from a normal cold. The first thing I noticed when Dr. Simon came into the room was that he was holding a large glass jug in one hand and a long tube with needles on both ends.

Moving past his nurse, Dr. Simon sat down at my side, lifting his stethoscope under my shirt to listened to my lungs. In the years that I had been coming to see Dr. Simon, I had never seen him move so quickly. "Hold up your hand," he said, attaching a small clip over my right forefinger. While waiting for the machine to analyze my oxygen statistics, Dr. Simon put a blood pressure cuff over my left arm. When the small device on my finger beeped, showing that my blood was low in oxygen, Dr. Simon glanced at Suzie. "His hematocrit is way too high and I'll have to bleed him. I need you to keep the pressure around his arm."

Suzie did as Dr. Simon asked and kept the blood pressure cuff tight while Dr. Simon rubbed my main vein with an alcohol swab. "So what is going on?" I asked.

"Your blood is way too thick and I need to drain it. Just lie back," Simon answered before quickly sliding the thick needle into my arm. It stung, but I was used to needles. As the tube filled with my blood, Dr. Simon pushed the other side into the glass jar, talking as my blood drained out of my body. "I've been monitoring your blood levels for months now, but last week your tests concerned me, so I had the lab run a few more tests. Long story short, your erythropoietin is over ten times the normal level and the mass and number of your red blood cells is far too high."

The relief I felt as my blood left my body was immense and I felt like a wave of energy was flowing into me. Even so, I could tell that Dr. Simon looked worried. "I know what EPO is," which I had quickly researched when studying the anabolic steroids, "So what is wrong? I thought a high EPO count was a good thing."

"Some athletes use blood doping or anabolic steroids to increase their erythropoietin levels, but most people test around four to eleven. Your test came back at sixty-nine. Although higher erythropoietin levels should enhance your endurance, when the number is that high, mixed with your red blood cell count it puts you at risk of stroke, heart attack and other issues. What you have is rare and not something I was expecting to see. We're just lucky that we caught it when we did." With my mother in the room, Dr. Simon was careful not to hint or give away that I was taking steroids.

"So you're saying that the anabolic steroids caused this?" I asked. Dr. Simon grew visibly uncomfortable with my mother in the room. "I told her everything, so you can be honest."

"At first I thought that was the case, but your numbers are so high that I believe you had a pre-existing issue. Although it is extremely rare, I went through your medical history and found that your red blood cell count has always been near a dangerous level. That is why I had your EPO tested and your red blood cells' mass tested. I was hoping I was wrong, but I believe you have always had what is called Secondary Polycythemia, or erythrocytosis. It can cause all your symptoms and due to the altitude you lived at combined with how active you are, the anabolic steroids exacerbated your condition. This means we have a major problem."

"So, I'm going to have to stop taking the anabolic steroids?" I asked, trying to remain calm but worried about giving up the one thing that had helped temper my mood swings.

"Well, we have two major problems. First of all, from all your mother has told me, somehow, your bipolar has continued to fade away, and your IBS and IGA haven't been problems since you began taking the steroids. I don't pretend to know why, but from everything I've heard, you're doing better than ever, so I'd prefer not to have you stop. However," Simon paused as he checked to see how full the jar was. "If you don't stop using them your condition will either remain the same, get worse or kill you. You're lucky you haven't already had a stroke or heart attack with your blood levels."

"I can't stop using them." I wasn't about to give up on the one thing that had improved my life. Not only had my skin cleared up, no longer needing Dapsone to keep my skin from blistering, but I was free of my IBS and my bipolar was continuing to improve. This all happened after I had started using anabolic steroids. To me, it seemed like too strong a coincidence to cast aside.

My mother had remained quiet since we got there, but she finally spoke up. "Simon, he really is getting better. If the steroids have helped, as odd as that might be, is there anything we can do to avoid having Kirk stop? What about lowering the dose?"

Simon checked the bottle and sat back in his chair, making sure my blood was still flowing. When the glass jar was half full, I felt my entire body relax. My cough vanished and my burning skin stopped itching. "I can keep drawing his blood when his numbers get too high, but there are serious risks to that approach. To be honest, I'm not sure I want Kirk to stop taking the steroids, but I see no other alternative."

Suddenly I remembered one study that I had read just recently that had a potential solution. "I read a study where a doctor was using a drug called Arimidex to raise men's testosterone instead of using anabolic steroids. Since I might not be able to keep taking testosterone, do you think that might be something worth trying?"

"Arimidex is an anti-estrogen," Simon said. He analyzed the idea aloud while he pumped up the cuff around my arm to tighten it just a bit. "Interesting, however, I don't think Arimidex could raise your testosterone in the same way. Also, we're not sure why the steroids are helping. When you first told me what you were doing, I would have bet my life that the steroids would've caused you to rocket into mania. Also, I can't write you a prescription for Arimidex."

When the glass jar was full, Simon removed the needle from my arm and bandaged the wound. I sat up, feeling better than I could express. "I promised you that I would never ask you to write a prescription. If I can get the Arimidex, do you think it's worth trying?"

Dr. Simon laughed and then caught himself before looking at my mother. "Your son is trying to give me a heart attack, isn't he?" Simon's joke had lightened the mood of the room. He turned a smiling gaze from me to my mother and back. "Your cough is gone, and you look much better. As for your idea, I can't stop you from doing anything, but at this point, I feel it would be risky to try anything new. I am against the use of anabolic steroids, but for you," Simon paused, not sure what to say. "I have no idea why they haven't made your bipolar worse, let alone better. I will monitor you and keep you safe, whatever decision you make under one condition. I don't want you doing anything on your own without consulting me and I want you to see another psychiatrist to monitor your bipolar. There is a chance that all this is simply a fluke and I will not let anything happen to you on my watch."

With that, Dr. Simon left the room and I stared forward. For the first time in my life, my bipolar was growing easier to deal with. Had I not taken the risk with the nandrolone decanoate for my IBS, I would be in the same miserable, uncontrollable roller coaster of deep depressions and violent manic episodes. I would make my decision, but I needed more research to support my decision.

As I began to walk out of the room, my mother stopped me. "What are you going to do?"

"I've come this far, and I'm not going back to the way I was. I know I still have swings, but I think trying the Arimidex is the best option. If it doesn't work, I can always go back."

V. RESEARCH AND TRIAL

After spending a few days looking for the same study that had shown Arimidex to be a possible alternative for men seeking testosterone replacement therapy, I became extremely frustrated. I did find some information that talked about it, but the original study had been removed. This was not uncommon, given that many studies did not have to publish their findings where others had to by law. I remembered the article well and the theory was sound, not like I had much of an option. Since the anabolic steroids, even at a lower dose, held greater risks for me than for other individuals, I knew that I had to give Arimidex a try. I had spent most of the money I had earned in the last month in order to secure a three-month supply of the real medication. It was extremely expensive, but I was finally living a better life, so I took the plunge.

Since the study I was interested in had been removed, I switched my research to the drug itself. As one of the more potent anti-estrogens on the market, it was a popular choice with athletes who were coming down off of a steroid cycle. The bodybuilders and athletes used the Arimidex to counteract a heavy steroid cycle, ensuring that there were no spikes in estrogen in an attempt to quickly boost their natural testosterone. Although there were some serious side effects for women, the drug had been designed for treating breast cancer when tamoxifen citrate was no longer effective. For men, there were also side effects, but most of the serious side effects were nothing compared to the bipolar medications that would eventually ruin my body.

The medical community itself kept itself safely away from anything to do with anabolic steroids due to all the controversy surrounding steroids and sports. In many ways, it made me angry because I felt, especially after my own experience, that the endocrine system had great potential for treating bipolar and perhaps other mental disorders. Not to mention that it had cleared up my IBS and my Linear IGA.

In the end, I knew that I had to give the Arimidex a chance. If it didn't work, I would go back to the anabolic steroids. To me, my life was worth risking to stave off the chaos that bipolar brought to every facet of my life. After letting Dr. Simon know what I was planning to do, promising that my mother and entire family would keep a close eye on me, I took my first dose: one milligram of Arimidex.

Although I had stopped taking the steroids, I still had to have my blood drawn every few weeks, missing only weeks when my iron was low. Dr. Simon had also prescribed oxygen for me to use when and if I felt it necessary. The only other option was to move away from Colorado and down to a lower altitude, but I couldn't uproot Nicoal as she had just been accepted to law school. At Dr. Simon's request, I did not change any of my bipolar medications. Everyone was worried about what might happen if I went cold turkey on the lithium and Lamictal.

After three weeks of being off of the steroids my IBS returned, however, it was less severe and painful than before and was very manageable. My skin had also remained smooth with no sign that the blisters would return. I truly believe that the steroids had helped me regain some stability, but the Arimidex was so much better.

Over the next few months I continued to have my blood taken when my red blood cell count rose too high and I needed daily oxygen to keep my blood under control. Although these were not good things to have to deal with, I would have given a limb or two for what was happening with my mind. Not only did my mood swings come less frequently, their intensity continued to lessen and my shattered mind, broken from years of delusions, depression and explosive manic episodes, was beginning to heal. The better I became, the more obvious to everyone that something was working. My psychiatrists and Dr. Simon were startled with my progress and had no explanations.

After a long while of watching me become more stable, Dr. Simon finally gave into my request to continue lowering my bipolar medications. With as much research as I had done, I still didn't know why the anabolic steroids had helped my bipolar, and even though I had made an educated choice to try Arimidex, Dr. Simon and I were both stumped as to why my bipolar continued to fade away.

After six months of titrating my bipolar medications, I found myself off all of my bipolar medications except my clonazepam used to treat my generalized anxiety. The fog that the medications had cast over my mind and all the side effects I had lived with for far too long were now gone. My mind was sharper and clearer. My hands were steadier. My energy level was increasing, and I looked forward to lifting and working out. Not only did my mood swings continue to fade away, but I began seeing life for the first time. The colors were brighter, but more importantly, I enjoyed them. Since I was a child, I had always said my favorite color was black, but as the world no longer felt dark and twisted, I found a sense of awe when looking at bright and vibrant colors. As I emerged from under the smothering blanket of bipolar, I was startled to learn what true happiness was.

Although it is strange to admit, there were some problems with being free of bipolar. I had lived my life in the present, unable to see or care about the world, others, or even myself in many respects. Without bipolar the filter that had kept me shielded from regular emotions was no longer there. I would like to think that I was brave, but the truth is that there was a terrifying learning curve to being 'normal'. My manic and depressive episodes that used to warp my world view were gone, forcing me to see myself and the truth of who I used to be.

PART FIVE: LIVING WITHOUT BIPOLAR

:: Learning How To Live and Love a Normal Life ::

I. STRUGGLING TO COPE WITH NORMALITY

After discontinuing the use of anabolic steroids and switching to the anti-estrogen, Arimidex, my mind that had once been broken and corrupted by bipolar was rapidly healing. I still remembered Dr. Smith telling me that I might not ever lead a normal life, even with the use of bipolar medications. I agreed with him in part, for out of the dozens of mood-stabilizing and anti-psychotic drugs I had tried, I hadn't been a functioning human being until after adding Arimidex to the mix.

I was still showing no symptoms of mania or depression after six months of taking the Arimidex. This was also as I had slowly weaned off all my bipolar medications. The only medication that I was using to stabilize my moods was Arimidex and it was amazing. Dr. Simon kept a close eye on me, still refusing to believe that my bipolar was in control until I remained stable for over a year. I didn't mind, for I was leading a normal life without bipolar swings and it was amazing.

What surprised me, however, was that the longer I remained stable the more aware of myself I became. As amazing as it was to see the world and myself clearly, it was also painful. Bipolar had protected me from seeing who I really was. Now that I had the freedom and ability to analyze myself, the more I realized who and what I used to be. To be candid, I wasn't ready to face my past or who I had been. In fact, I really wasn't prepared for being normal.

All my life, I had lived without fear while my other emotions had always been twisted by my swings. I had been unable to listen to anyone giving me advice because I truly thought I was better than others. Relationships had been ruined by my warped view of situations and I had thought of no one but myself. The sharper and more stable my mind became, the less I liked who I used to be. Seeing the world like others did was not always easy, but I was willing to change, for anything was better than my old life.

Although I was doing well, Dr. Simon, my psychiatrists and family continued to watch me carefully, worried that my recovery had been a fluke. Without a shred of scientific data or a single study to support using an anti-estrogen as a mood-stabilizer, everyone expected me to crash. I wasn't worried, however; I was living for the first time without bipolar distorting my vision. What I saw and felt on a daily basis only confirmed that I was getting better, which I had no way of explaining, for it was a new experience for me and I was the only one living it.

Because everyone expected me to crash, if I had a hard day and felt grumpy, or had a great day that raised my spirits, they all would ask me if I had taken my medication and if I was okay. I disliked the question and it took me time to realize that the only reason my family asked was because they cared. What startled me was that until then, I had not really understood how much I was loved. Even my perception of love had been distorted by bipolar.

As I struggled to understand all the changes I was going through and as I got better I never thought that my family would have a hard time adjusting to the new me. Now free of my wild swings, I was more focused and calmer than ever before. It was strange to discover that I was not the comedian I thought I was but was actually a very serious and passionate person. My manic episodes had always deluded me into believing that I was a carefree joker, but the truth was that it was the bipolar swings that made me carefree. It was strange to realize I didn't even know who I really was, but interesting to discover.

My recovery did not only affect me. My mother was so used to taking care of me when I wasn't able to take care of myself, she would prepare food for me without knowing that I had already made myself lunch. She was constantly prepared to drive me places, and she shared both relief and some disappointment when I could make the drives myself.

It wasn't only my mother who was having a hard time adjusting to the absence of my bipolar. In fact, everyone I was close with had formed some way to cope with my irrational explosions and deep depressions. My sister, used to trying to lift my spirits when I was down, continued to spend her hard-earned money buying me gifts while my father found it strange when

I joined everyone at the dinner table and talked instead of vanishing into the basement. The first time I asked my father how his day had been made his eyes widen with shock, making me realize that I had never taken an interest in anyone's life but my own.

Out of everyone, my wife had a very hard time adjusting to my stability. Although she was used to seeing both my mania and depression, she focused on our best moments which always took place when I was first becoming manic. Like everyone that was close to me, Nicoal had blocked out many of our worst times and clung to the memories when I couldn't stop laughing, joking or telling funny stories. With no more mania, I didn't laugh or joke the way I had when in the beginning stages of my manic episodes. This led my wife to constantly doubt my happiness. No longer imbalanced and truly happy for the first time in my life, I realized that no matter how many times I tried to explain that I was happy, it would take time for everyone to adjust to the new me. The hardest part for me was being reminded of who I used to be and facing the fact that my instability had forced the people I loved to change their life in an attempt to survive living with me.

One thing was clear about my situation: there was no one to help guide me. I read countless memoirs and books about bipolar, but I couldn't find anyone who was in the same situation. Even though I knew my wife, family and friends loved me, I felt very alone at times and knew that I would have to adapt to a 'normal' life without a mentor or a role model. After tasting what real stability was like, I didn't think I could survive if my bipolar returned. The only problem, however, was that the Arimidex was expensive. Since I was getting the hospital grade medication from a source I promised never to divulge, the medication was even more expensive than from a pharmacy. Not only was I faced with the challenge of understanding my new life, but my recovery was being threatened for the first time as I realized I couldn't afford to continue taking the medication.

The situation was plainly untenable, and knowing this, I was desperate to find a solution. I used that tried and trusted method once more and began researching other anti-estrogens.

When I contacted them to see if there was any way I could get the Arimidex at a lower cost, my source suggested that I take a look at a drug called tamoxifen citrate. With tamoxifen citrate also being an anti-estrogen at a fraction of the price, I used all my spare time to research the drug. Although tamoxifen citrate was also used in the treatment of breast cancer, it had a different way of lowering the estrogen in my body. What surprised me was reading the comments left by bodybuilders who had tried taking a break from their steroids without using tamoxifen citrate or Arimidex. Many of them reported feeling depressed, crying and even contemplating suicide. The reports of the men that had used the tamoxifen citrate, however, did not suffer from depression. Since my mind was finally beginning to heal, I didn't want to take any risks, but I was quickly running out of money and needed to make a decision before I ran out of my Arimidex.

I wasn't about to make any more medical decisions before consulting Dr. Simon. I scheduled an appointment with him a few days later. Although I had caused my body considerable harm with my self-experimentation, Dr. Simon had slowly begun to trust my research and respect my mind and ideas. Even after watching my bipolar vanish, he fully admitted that the medical professional inside him was not ready to accept that Arimidex had stabilized my moods, as there was no medical study to back such a conclusion. In fact, out of everyone in my life, he was perhaps the most concerned that my bipolar would come back.

After signing in, filling out paperwork and being brought back to one of the exam rooms, I sat down on the examination table and suddenly realized that it was the first time I had come to the doctor by myself. It was certainly the first time I had ever filled out any paperwork. To most people, this would not be a big deal. It was a startling realization to think about how far I'd come, and how many steps I still had to go toward ultimate self-sufficiency.

Simon walked into the room and sat down. "I just talked with your psychiatrist and your family. Everyone says that you feel and act like a completely different person, but the truth is that I'm worried. You realize that we aren't out of the woods yet, don't you?" I nodded, knowing that six months, although a long time to me, was not enough for any medical professional to take seriously. "So, have you had any dark thoughts or felt even a bit manic?"

"I've been doing really well," I answered truthfully. "I've been saving as much money as I can. I haven't missed a day of work and as for my moods..." I paused for a second, realizing that I truly was aware of my moods. I didn't have to think if I had felt any depression or mania. I knew that I hadn't. "...the bipolar is gone."

"I have been practicing medicine since your mother was a child and I can honestly say that you are the first true mystery that has walked into my office." Dr. Simon wasn't smiling as he added, "And I'm not fond of mysteries." Dr. Simon ran his hand through his thin gray hair and got down to business. "So, what did you want to talk to me about?"

"I've been researching another anti-estrogen."

Dr. Simon cut me off before I could finish. "The Arimidex appears to be working, why are you still researching?"

"I'd prefer not to stop taking the Arimidex, but I don't think I can afford the medication." Simon sighed, understanding where I was coming from, and I continued. "The drug I've been researching is much cheaper than Arimidex and it's actually been used in official trials to treat mania. There are no studies that show it works as a mood stabilizer, but I've read enough to believe it might work just as well as the Arimidex."

"And what were the results of the trials?"

"They were not conclusive, but not completely negative." I explained what I had found, stated my case and waited for Dr. Simon to respond.

Simon gave another small sigh. "Tamoxifen is another anti-estrogen used to treat breast cancer and I still don't have a clue as to why Arimidex has helped you. Do you really want to risk your stability by changing anything?"

I was about to answer when an odd sensation washed over me. Over the past few months as my mind grew sharper and my life was finally getting back on track, there were moments where I was overcome by emotions that I didn't understand and had never felt before. I knew in theory what anger, joy, fear and sadness were, but the truth was that I had never truly experienced any real emotions until recently. While learning to deal with a new and normal life, understanding and handling new and unfamiliar emotions was the most trying and difficult challenge that I faced.

Simon just sat there, waiting for me to answer as I tried to figure out what I was feeling. All my life, decisions had been easy. I had lived without any fear or regret to hold me back from making rash choices, so when I wasn't able to immediately answer, I felt confused. What I was really feeling, however, was doubt and fear. I didn't know it at the time, but I did know that I didn't like it. I took a shaky breath and finally answered. "I don't want to risk anything, but money is tight, and I don't have a choice. I can get tamoxifen from the same person that is supplying the Arimidex. Honestly, I don't know..." I paused again, frustrated that I was having a hard time deciding on what was best. I had done my research and felt like tamoxifen citrate was the right choice, but I kept wondering what might happen if I was wrong. Overwhelmed with new, unfamiliar emotions that I was not equipped to deal with, I wondered if something was wrong.

Dr. Simon was watching me closely, analyzing my hesitation which I had never displayed before. "Do you think it is the smart choice? I have been against every move you have made, but you have done well. If you're feeling doubt, just know I'll support whatever decision you make and monitor you. If the tamoxifen doesn't work as well, you call me at the first sign of trouble. Don't wait, do you understand?"

"I do," I said, and the doubt vanished. I had never been an emotional person, so I didn't understand why Dr. Simon's words had meant so much to me. My ego had always had two settings, making me believe that I was god-like or worthless. Dr. Simon's statement had boosted my confidence a bit and I liked that. "I'll get the tamoxifen and call you before I change anything."

Dr. Simon nodded. "I want you to give me a call whenever you need to. Do you have my cell phone?"

I knew that Dr. Simon kept his cell phone number secret, as all doctors needed and deserved some personal time and privacy, so when he asked and I said, "No," I felt honored when he wrote it down on a slip of paper and handed it to me.

"Call me if anything changes."

"I will." His words, his reassurance and his concern all made me smile. Somehow, even though I had caused Dr. Simon more worry than he ever deserved, I had earned his respect. I knew he was still waiting for things to go south, but that wasn't going to happen. I may have felt doubt about trying something other than Arimidex, but I had no doubt that my mind was healing. If it was indeed the anti-estrogen that had freed me from bipolar, then I had to believe that the tamoxifen would also work.

After saying goodbye to Bonnie, Suzie and Simon, I left the office and walked to my car. The air was fresh, and the cool breeze lightly stung my cheeks. Even though Dr. Simon had given me the green light for switching from the Arimidex to the tamoxifen citrate, I couldn't shake the vision of who I used to be. For the first time in my life, doubt and fear had appeared, creeping into my life. They were totally unwelcome, making me wonder if there was a way I could make more money to stay on the Arimidex. In the past I had made life-changing decisions without a second thought, but now that I was balanced, I was struggling to trust my own research.

I got into the car, put my seat belt on, and brought my hands to my face. I had never realized that bipolar had protected me from a whole spectrum of emotions, both positive and negative. Those I had felt when manic or depressed had always been twisted, extreme, and fleeting, but the doubt I felt that day was like a splinter I couldn't pluck from my mind. Throughout my life, I had never felt doubt. When depressed I was certain that I was worthless and undeserving of the right to live, and while manic there were no second guesses: I was impulsive, righteous, a supreme genius waiting for everyone to realize the fact. Now I had doubt, and I didn't like it.

Ever since I started taking the Arimidex my brain had grown sharper, more stable and calmer, so feeling overwhelmed internally, especially in ways I didn't recognize, was disconcerting. Because I was growing more aware of myself with each passing day I had grown to believe that I knew how to control my emotions. The truth, however, was that I had never experienced real or normal emotions. Until Arimidex, I had lived in my own world while my bipolar shielded me from emotions and reality. I might have been free of bipolar, but I quickly realized that I had a long way to go before I could claim a full recovery.

With a deep, steadying breath, I started the car and turned the radio on. Although I couldn't shake the self-doubt I was feeling, I knew that I would eventually have to make a decision. When I returned home, I made a call to my contact and ordered a two-month supply of tamoxifen citrate. I wasn't sure if I would try it or not, but I figured I couldn't make a decision until I had some in hand.

A week later, this Arimidex substitute arrived in the mail. My father walked into the kitchen, seeing me holding a bottle of Arimidex in one hand and tamoxifen citrate in the other. Intellectually I understood the definitions and effects of every human emotion, but I was finally beginning to feel them. I must admit that knowing about them and experiencing them are completely different. "What are you doing?"

I turned to look at my father, answering him truthfully. "I can't make up my mind." I sighed, frustrated that I couldn't make a decision. It was the first time I could remember struggling to commit. "I don't get it, Dad. I did my research, but I keep wondering if I'm wrong."

My father walked over and studied both medications before patting me on my shoulder. "Son, it's normal to doubt and worry, especially when your life is finally coming together." Ever since talking with Dr. Simon about switching medications I had been struggling to identify what I was feeling.

Since I had never worried about myself, others or my actions, my father's analysis of my emotions hit home.

"How do I make such a big decision when I feel the way I do?"

Sensing that I was confused, my dad took both bottles of medication out of my hands and placed them on the kitchen counter. "Everyone deals with doubt and fear, son, you just can't let it control you. I can't tell you what to do, but I can tell you to trust your research and your gut. If the tamoxifen doesn't work as well, you can always switch back and I'll help pay for it if I can." At the time, my parents were struggling, so his offer was beyond generous.

I didn't want to risk my stability, but I was also aware that I couldn't continue to pay for the Arimidex. In the past I would not have hesitated to try the tamoxifen, but I was a different person now. Stable and aware of how my decision could affect everyone I cared for, I just stood there staring at both medications. I believed that the tamoxifen citrate would work, but the more I researched, the clearer it was that there were no studies or data to support using any anti-estrogen in place of a mood stabilizer. With no way to know if the tamoxifen citrate would be as effective as the Arimidex I knew I would eventually have to make a decision.

For the first time since starting Arimidex I encountered a moment that would have been easier to handle when I was still suffering from bipolar. I didn't miss being bipolar because every aspect of my life was better when normal but realizing how emotionally stunted I was surprised me.

Tired of being overwhelmed by self-doubt and fear, I repeated my father's words. "I can always switch back to the Arimidex." With that, I lifted the bottle of tamoxifen citrate from the counter, opened the bottle and tipped it until a single tablet fell into my palm. I couldn't afford the Arimidex and if there was even a chance that the tamoxifen citrate worked, I owed it to my wife and myself to try. Taking the pill made my decision was final, and although I would keep the Arimidex close by in case I began to slip, I felt the doubt that had been haunting me for the past week fade away. "Thanks for the talk, pops."

"Any time," he said with a gentle smile before walking away, leaving me alone in the kitchen. It had never been clearer that adapting to normal life was going to be far more difficult than I first thought, but in many ways, as much as I hated feeling doubt or fear, I loved the truth of this new situation in my heart and mind. I had lived a sheltered life for far too long and I was ready to grow up and experience the world the way I was supposed to.

***

Switching to tamoxifen citrate had been a calculated risk that had worried everyone, but after two months of taking the medication and remaining stable, everyone, was growing increasingly confident that I had made the right choice. This included Dr. Simon, the most ardent skeptic in my inner circle. Although the two medications had very different methods of reducing the body's estrogen, they both worked. How they worked, however, was still a mystery that I wanted to solve. The only problem was that as much as I wanted to research, I was dealing with a whole new set of problems. These included facing my past and brightening into a person who could fully feel all life had to offer. It was a new and often frustrating double-edged sword.

I quickly found that there was an enormous difference between understanding the definitions of positive and negative emotions and actually experiencing them. As I continued to grow more stable and self-aware, I quickly realized that my understanding of what they were had been twisted or blocked by my bipolar. I might have been turning twenty-nine, but I was experiencing life and feelings for the first time. Knowing that I had to face and master the overwhelming, the disappointing, the passionate, the fervent, the vehement and despondent that I'd never had to really deal with in the past. This continued to surprise me, and I prepared as best I could. It was more challenging than I had ever imagined.

II. FACING AND EXPERIENCING REAL EMOTIONS

It is, and always will be, strange for me to look back and realize that all my life I had never experienced real emotions. I use the word 'real', because I can't think of a better word. It wasn't that I hadn't felt anger, hatred or bliss, for at the peaks of my mania or depression I had certainly acted out those emotions, but they had always been tainted and exaggerated by my twisted reality. As my mind grew sharper and more self-aware, I began to realize that I had never truly enjoyed watching a movie, opening presents, looking at the stars, or even relationships. Even though I realized that every memory involving emotion was distorted, I still wasn't prepared for how my newly normal mind would experience and deal with it all.

Some, like joy, happiness and love were strong enough to make my eyes tear up and I admit that it was always easier to handle the positive. They were indescribably vivid, impacting, true and alluring. Every time I laughed, the world seemed brighter and warmer. In many ways I was like a child, overwhelmed and surprised with how powerful a calm and free mind experienced emotions. Even though the negative ones like stress, fear, anger and doubt, were much harder to manage and control, mostly because they made me feel horrible, *feeling* real emotions, bad or good, was intoxicating. Since bipolar had only allowed me to taste the most extreme of these, realizing how broad and varied real emotions were was very daunting and exciting.

For a time I was doing well, learning to let go of anger and enjoy the positive, but when I was first hit with regret I was truly overwhelmed. Hate and love seemed easy to understand compared to regret. Out of all the poor choices I had made in my life, bipolar had always kept me from looking back. Knowing there was no way to understand and accept my past without delving into it with an open mind, I was forced to look at the animal I used to be. It was more painful than I like to admit.

Now free of bipolar and able to look at my past and future with a startling clarity and understanding, I was very aware that I had never been in control. Yet knowing that I was not thinking with a normal mind during many of my most radical choices and actions did not lessen the guilt, pain and horror I felt when looking at my past. Sober from my bipolar, my past was extremely painful to reflect upon. I had ruined countless friendships, demolished all but one romantic relationship and passed up some amazing financial opportunities during my life and knowing that was hard to take. At least my swings kept me from understanding the impact of my actions. Eventually, I realized that I had one of two choices; I could let my past overwhelm me, letting my regret overrun my life, or I could let go of my past and appreciate the good and the bad that had led me to where I was: stable, successful, married and happy.

Unlike many of the new emotions I was experiencing, I couldn't sit back and let go of the regret I felt. I needed to take action, so I made a list of everyone that I had wronged and began making calls. During my calls to more people than I like to admit, I never talked about bipolar, focusing only on apologizing for my actions. Some of the calls were extremely hard to make, but every time someone forgave me I felt a slight weight slide from my shoulders. I was looking for two things: forgiveness for my actions and the ability to start a new life that I was proud of. It took a long time but eventually I began to accept my old life as part of who I was. Although I could never make up for what I put my family and friends through, I was committed to trying. Finally learning how to let go of my regrets was a big step for me, helping me to understand who I used to be, who I wanted to be, and that I was lucky to be alive.

As I continued to get better at recognizing, analyzing and reacting calmly to the constant stream of new feelings, the more I appreciated being free of bipolar. Although bipolar protected me from many of the negative emotions and left me free to act without fear, doubt or regret, feeling something real was so much more fulfilling. It had taken twenty-nine years to feel alive, but it was worth the wait. Life was so much sweeter after knowing what it felt like to be ruled by rash thoughts and violent actions.

I was bipolar free and although life wasn't always easy, I loved it. If I die early from the damage I caused to my body during my research, I would gladly trade my remaining life for the few years that I have recently been blessed to live.

III. EVOLVING RELATIONSHIP DYNAMICS

I knew that I had been a horrible person, so my life was now centered around kindness and understanding. Although there were brief moments when I was kind and thoughtful in my past, they were so rare that I felt the need to catch up. Living only for myself, it wasn't a surprise that the list of people that had put up with me was extremely short. During my life I had chased away so many great people, terrifying some and breaking the hearts of others, I wanted to make those who still stood by me proud. The first real problem I found about trying to be a good person was that I had established bad habits.

Due to the paranoia I experienced during my manic episodes I had developed a sense that everyone was trying to weasel something out of me, or against me. Since I was always looking out only for myself, it was no surprise that I had thought others worked the same way. Some of my habits that I had developed for self-preservation were hard to unlearn. Lying, for example, was second nature and I had honed my ability to read and manipulate others before they could do the same to me. My dark view of the world had turned me into a horrible person, but I now had a second chance.

After finally learning to manage this flood of new and pure emotions with some level of understanding, it was frustrating when my old habits subconsciously lashed out. It felt as if every time I was getting the knack of being normal, a new twist or surprise would catch me off guard. I admit that no one can be perfect, but I was just trying to be better and it was surprisingly hard. Even after more than a full year without a hint of bipolar showing through, I still caught myself manipulating my relationships. In the past, I had done so because I believed it was an act of survival. Now I knew better. This made it infuriating that lying and manipulating had become instinctual. I didn't want to lie anymore, for there was no need and I wanted nothing more than to be a good person.

When I was a child, I remember that one of my best friends had a problem with cursing, so his mother made him put a penny in a jar every time he cursed. It had worked for my friend, so I figured that I would start a jar, adding a dollar whenever I caught myself manipulating, lying or even gossiping. Needless to say, the jar filled up quickly as I struggled to change the person bipolar had molded me into. My determination never wavered, however, and unlike the past when mania sent my brain into overdrive or depression held me back, I felt focused and in control. It was finally possible to change.

Very aware of the person I used to be and how bipolar had affected me, I did not like knowing that every action I had ever taken had been done with the sole intent of personal gain. I was slowly fixing the way I treated others, but it hit me that I was still doing it for myself. For so long, I had been oblivious to other peoples' needs that I hadn't even thought about becoming better at being a more giving individual. I certainly knew how to read others, so I decided to use that ability to help those I cared about. After spending my life feeding off of others I felt it was my turn to give back.

The better I became at understanding my own motives, the needs of my friends, family and wife, the better and more enjoyable each relationship became. Day by day I was growing kinder and gentler, slowly polishing the person I used to be into something I would be proud of. I was also working to be a better son, brother, friend and husband. I admit that I made mistakes, but the more effort I put in the more all of my relationships, both personal and professional, strengthened.

That year was the first time I had acted in a selfless way without consciously thinking about it. My mother had made quite a feast for Thanksgiving and for the first time I had enjoyed the holiday, eating with everyone and talking instead of hiding in my room, avoiding conversation. Seeing how happy everyone was made me realize that I had never truly enjoyed holidays or vacations. Worse, I realized that I had viewed them as obligations that I was forced into, typically ruining every time our family did something together. Even Christmas, regardless if I was manic or depressed, always felt like a chore. Of course I looked forward to opening presents, but there were only so many presents. And, when I was done opening my gifts, I would disappear in my room, playing by myself. Thinking back, I rarely showed any appreciation for the gifts that I had been given. However, that year I was looking forward to Christmas, and not because I wanted something, but because I had gone shopping for everyone else for the first time in my life and was excited to give everyone their gifts.

When I say that I had never gone shopping for someone else, I'm sad to admit that I can only think of three gifts that I had gone out and purchased for someone else. There was the engagement ring for my wife, a pearl necklace I had bought my sister when I was in high school and a small stuffed animal for my mother. All the gifts that had supposedly come from me, my mother had picked out and wrapped for me every Christmas. Intent on making our family holiday special, I had even purchased tags, bows, ribbon and wrapping paper. However, since I had never wrapped a present before, I didn't do the best job. Although my presents looked wrapped by a two-year-old, I didn't care. It was also the first Christmas since I had been free of bipolar.

Three days after Thanksgiving I waited patiently for everyone to go to bed. After making sure Nicoal was asleep, I carefully crawled out of bed, quietly grabbing my bag of poorly wrapped presents from my closet before heading upstairs. I then set the bag down and tiptoed through the kitchen and quietly entered the garage.

Since I was a child, we had always kept our artificial Christmas tree in the garage. It was carefully and tightly wrapped in a large box that was long and wide, making it difficult to carry alone. I had watched my mother and father take out the tree every year but couldn't remember ever helping without throwing a fit. It never even dawned on me that had I been helping every year, my mother and father wouldn't have needed to work so hard. This year would be different.

I hoisted it over my shoulder before carefully and quietly walking back inside, I nearly slipped on the kitchen floor, but caught myself. I opened the box as quietly as I could, pulled out each piece of the tree, checking that the wires weren't tangled. Piece by piece, I assembled the tree, checking to make sure it wasn't off center. I wanted everything to be perfect and was determined to make it happen. The entire time I was putting the tree together I had a silly grin on my face as it was the first time I was excited to decorate the tree and stack presents beneath it. I was even more excited to surprise my family and wife.

When I was finished, I stood there, finally understanding the magic of the holidays. It wasn't about presents or getting what I wanted, nor was it an obligation. The holidays were about appreciating everything I had and showing compassion and love to those I cared for. Cleaning up the box and putting it back into the garage, I had one thing left to do. Bringing my bag of presents over to the tree, I carefully placed the gifts I had personally wrapped under the tree.

I stepped back to admire my handiwork with that same lopsided grin. The joy I felt quickly faded as I realized it was the first time I had done something wonderful without first having an agenda. My mind swirled with memories of the past; the moment was bittersweet. I found that I couldn't think of a single vacation or holiday that I had not ruined for my family. I wanted to believe that I was mistaken, but I knew I wasn't. The worst of the Christmas memories almost brought me to tears. I had been twelve and before even opening my first present, I had lost my temper for a reason I couldn't remember. What stood out in my mind was that I had told my mother, father and sister that I hated them before knocking over the tree and breaking my mother's favorite ornament.

I sat on the floor, overwhelmed at the idea that I could have ever been so cruel, eyes locked on the tall Christmas tree and its tip which was lit by the gentle moonlight shining in through our front windows. I wondered through the thick haze of guilt if there would ever come a time when I could forgive myself for what I had done to those I cared most about.

"What are you doing up..." I heard my mother ask from the top of the stairs.. Her voice quickly faded away as she looked down and saw me sitting in front of the tree. "You put up the tree."

I looked up and nodded, realizing that her voice had shaken as she spoke. She wasn't upset that I had awakened her, she was shocked at what she was looking at. "It was supposed to be a surprise, but since you're up, you want to hang the first ornament?"

My mother stood there for a long while, staring first at the tree and then back to me. After a long pause, she realized that I had asked her a question and nodded quickly before walking quietly down the stairs. Since it was late and I was hardly sleepy, I expected her to ask if I was feeling a bit manic, but she simply walked over to me and reached out, repeating what she had already said, "You put up the tree."

"Yes," I responded, and gave my mother a big hug. "I just thought I would get it done so everyone else could just enjoy it."

She let go of me and walked over to the tree, noticing the presents I had set out sitting around the base. When she turned back around, my mother's eyes were brimming with tears. "You've never put up the tree before," she said, then pointed to the presents, adding: "and the presents."

Although I didn't want to, when I saw my mother next to the tree with her eyes filled with tears, all I could think of was that I had broken the ornament that she had enjoyed since she was a child. With both of her parents passing away when she was young, that ornament was not replaceable. Needing to escape from the guilt I felt, I walked over to my mom, putting my hand on her shoulder as she stared at the tree with child-like awe. "I'm sorry that I broke your ornament."

But she just laughed and cried and looked at me as if I were a different person. I was. I am. Her tear-streaked face was bright and filled with joy. "I don't care. This is worth a thousand ornaments."

I hadn't known how much my mother had wanted me to enjoy holidays and birthdays, but in the midst of her crying tears of joy and taking hold of me, I felt my past vanish, if only for that moment. At that moment, even though I was still struggling to understand who I was, I knew that it felt good to bring joy to others. It may have taken me twenty-nine years to give my family the Christmas they deserved, but I figured it was better late than never.

The next day, everyone was in good spirits, but the revelation that I had not a single memory where I had not ruined an important occasion was still bitter. I refused to let my past ruin the day, and instead put on a smile and swore that I would continue getting better. I had only been normal for a year and I felt like a child experiencing everything for the first time, but that wouldn't stop me from becoming a good man. Aware that I was a work in progress, I was finally beginning to understand who I wanted to be, memories I wanted to create, legacies to share, and accomplishments that needed to be happening.

IV. A SECOND CHANCE AND A NEW PURPOSE

Long before I had begun taking Arimidex my mother had talked me into going to a few bipolar support groups. I had been against the idea, thinking that I was too good to waste my time talking about my problems with a bunch of strangers. After a few weeks of refusing to try, I gave in. To my surprise, I ended up making quite a few friends. One of the people, I'll call him Dave, had so much in common with me that we became quite close. Dave, like me, was suffering from an extreme case of bipolar and we shared many of the same passions and problems. Neither of us could hold a job or keep ourselves from sabotaging our romantic relationships. Dave was four years older than I and I now know that he was a reflection of my future.

Dave was missing his top teeth due to a bar fight, and his stories and struggles were always familiar, but somehow I had avoided jail and many other unpleasant events while Dave hadn't. Like me, Dave's manias would tear his world apart, only he was always caught and punished while I had somehow escaped unscathed from similar situations. For a time, Dave and I were very close, but when I began getting better our commonalities began to vanish. After six months of taking Arimidex, Dave and the others in the bipolar group would ask me what medications I was taking, seeing how well

I was doing and wanting to gain some form of control. I remembered the desperation they felt. No one wants to suffer from bipolar and everyone in the group, especially the more severe cases like Dave and myself, were always searching for answers and the ability to live a normal life. As much as I wanted to tell everyone what I was taking and what I had discovered, I didn't want anyone to take the same risks that had almost killed me. I also had no idea if it would work on others, although I believed in my research and thought there was true potential.

As time went on and the bipolar that had ruled my life continued to vanish, I was never more aware of the second chance I had been given than when I was talking with Dave. While my life and relationships continued to heal and improve, Dave's life was being eaten away due to his bipolar. Every time he lost another job due to his mania or he flew to another country believing he was too important to live in normal society, it was like I was looking into a mirror of my past. I do not like to use the words insane or crazy, but the more my mind healed the more I realized just how insane I used to be. Watching Dave made me wonder why I had been given a second chance when everyone else I knew who was bipolar was suffering. I had been a selfish, egotistical and delusional monster caring only about myself, making me feel like I didn't deserve a second chance.

When Dave flew to California, believing he had figured out a new math that would change the world, I knew that I couldn't keep my discovery a secret. I didn't deserve a chance to reinvent myself while I watched others just like me continue to self-destruct. Since I had been given a second chance, I wasn't about to squander it. Somehow, I had to figure out if my discovery would work on others suffering from bipolar, but with no credentials, I was just another bipolar individual that would sound completely delusional if I tried to tell any professional that I had found a cure that science insisted did not exist.

Knowing that no one would listen to me, I called the only person I thought could help. After a long discussion with Dr. Simon on the phone, he had agreed to meet with me. To this day, I still believe that Dr. Simon wanted to get to the bottom of my cure as badly as I did. Although he had been skeptical at first, I was approaching him after eighteen months of stability, making my recovery more medically valid and yet still mysterious.

Later that week I drove to Simon's office and we sat down in private to talk. Dr. Simon had become a friend and a mentor, but more importantly, he was the only person that had seen my recovery. Unlike my psychiatrists,

Dr. Simon had seen me more often and was the only one I had entrusted with every risk and experiment I had tried in a desperate attempt to heal my broken mind. As we both sat down, he straightened his tie and smiled. "You're looking good," he said, gesturing to my button down shirt and slacks. "You realize that only a year ago I never saw you cleanly shaven or wearing anything but sweats." Dr. Simon brushed back his thinning silver hair and asked, "So, why did you want to meet?"

Before I answered, I subconsciously reached up to touch my face. I was cleanly shaven and well dressed. I had been so focused on my stability and mental health that I had never thought about my appearance, but Dr. Simon was right. Not only did I keep myself clean, but I dressed better, stood tall and appeared confident. I simply wasn't the same person any longer. "Well, I'm not sure how to start," I began, deciding to simply dive in and ask. "I believe that the Arimidex or tamoxifen citrate will work on other people suffering from bipolar. However, with no credentials, I would just sound crazy. So, to cut to the chase, I need help proving that I'm right. I want to help people escape bipolar so they can live a fulfilling life."

Dr. Simon's smile flattened as he met my eyes with his own. "There is a possibility that the anti-estrogens would work on others, but legally I can't do anything. I'd like to, but the liability is beyond what I can support."

I had come prepared for this and extracted a folder from the briefcase at my side. I handed it to Dr. Simon and let him read before I explained. When I realized that I couldn't keep my recovery a secret, I had seen a lawyer, asking what possible options Dr. Simon might have. The lawyer had drawn up consent forms, explaining that Dr. Simon could use them to treat someone that had tried everything and had run out of options. Although it wouldn't be considered clinical data, if we could build up enough case studies, showing that the medication worked, perhaps we would have a chance to get a clinical trial started. "I spoke to a lawyer before coming to meet you. If someone is suffering from bipolar and they are out of options, you can legally prescribe tamoxifen or Arimidex as long as they are fully informed of all potential risks and sign the informed consent form."

Dr. Simon looked over the papers and sighed before looking back at me. "Let me ask you something."

"Sure," I said as I nodded. "Shoot."

"I admit that you have surprised me, but I must ask, when you are finally stable and your professional and personal life are beginning to come together, why are you interested in trying your method of treating bipolar on anyone else?"

It was a fair question and I was surprised how easily my answer came. "Because, now that I am better, I can't stand by and watch others suffer as I did. If there is even a chance that the anti-estrogens could work on others, I couldn't live with myself if I didn't try. I am willing to help in any way I can, but I can't do it on my own."

Dr. Simon looked out the window and took a deep breath before returning his gaze to me. "I need to talk to my lawyer and get more detailed information, but I will see what I can do. You understand that I'm not promising anything, don't you?"

"I do," I said, and stood. I was aware of the stress I had caused Dr. Simon when I had first begun to experiment and I certainly wasn't going to push him now, especially after all he had done for me. "Thanks for everything," I added, and reached out to shake his hand.

***

A month later, Dr. Simon had begun to treat a few extreme cases of bipolar with tamoxifen citrate. He would have prescribed Arimidex, but because Dr. Simon was seeing the patients for free and providing the medication, he chose tamoxifen citrate because of its low cost. Together, Dr. Simon and I decided that we would approach treating others just as we had approached my own treatment. Each patient that Dr. Simon wrote a prescription for had to be officially diagnosed with bipolar and working with a trained psychiatrist as that was not Dr. Simon's expertise and, as always, he only wanted his patients to be safe.

Most importantly, each subject that began using tamoxifen citrate *had* to continue taking their bipolar medications, not cutting the dose unless first talking to Dr. Simon. Dr. Simon also required the patient, as well as someone they lived with, to keep a mood and medication chart. Dr. Simon had also given each patient and their family members my phone number, explaining that I was the first person to have tried using an anti-estrogen as a mood stabilizer. Due to the unique position I was in, Dr. Simon wanted me to be available to coach the families and patients since I was the only one with the personal experience. I had to follow the same rules as a doctor when it came to privacy, but I was trained to not give any medical advice and if it was needed, to have the family or patient immediately contact Dr. Simon or their psychiatrist.

Every patient who was working with Dr. Simon was experiencing some added stability, but as each patient slowly lowered their other medications, the patient and their family members would call me with questions as all the patients began to improve. Although everyone was told that I had no medical or counseling degree, the family members and patients preferred to talk to me, not because they didn't like Dr. Simon, but because they knew I understood what they were going through. After suffering for years with bipolar only to have fully recovered, I understood exactly what each person was going through, but more importantly, I could explain the patients' moods, triggers and actions in a way that made sense to both the patient and the family members that called to talk to me. The first time I was able to help a family find some understanding of bipolar and how it affects the mind I knew why I had been given a second chance. I wanted to help everyone find the peace and joy I now lived with.

As time went on, the patients continued to improve and many of them told others about Dr. Simon and myself. Three years later, Dr. Simon and I both knew that there was a definite connection between the endocrine system and bipolar. Not only were many of the patients living a stable life without taking any traditional bipolar medications, but they were excelling at life. The only problems they had were about dealing with normal emotions and stability. Like I, they struggled to understand their life and mind once the bipolar was retreating and their medications no longer dulled their minds. Luckily, I had already gone through each of their steps, able to help them understand what being new to normal was like.

After spending countless hours talking and explaining things to the patients, family and doctors that wanted to talk with me, I was asked to write the story of how I overcame bipolar. Seeing how well the anti-estrogens worked, Dr. Simon and I were convinced that we weren't just imagining that the new method worked, and so were the families and patients who still continue to improve. After coaching families and their bipolar spouses, siblings or children, I decided that my story was worth writing. As much as I hope my book causes a stir in the medical world, I feel blessed every day that I somehow escaped bipolar and am now helping others do the same. To everyone who has ever dealt, directly or indirectly, with bipolar, I hope with all my heart that my story instills a sense of hope.

There is a cure, and everyone can have a second chance.

EPILOGUE
FIFTEEN YEARS LATER

Over fifteen years ago I began an untested medication protocol to treat the bipolar that was tearing my mind and life apart. It was a desperate attempt to save my mind, heart, and soul from the darkness that was consuming me. My life had been falling apart with each passing moment. Relationships failed, friends fled, loved ones gave up hope, well-meaning medical professionals tempered my expectations, and my last memory of college was being so medicated and depressed I was unable to write my own name on my mid-term. In short, the failures were growing so heavy that I was losing sight of why I should fight onwards.

Now, nearly nine years after my memoir was published, I write this epilogue for every person, loved one, family member, or life-partner that is struggling with mental health. I let well-meaning medical professionals convince me that my potential was limited. I let the world around me beat me down, yet within me was a single ember of hope that refused to die out. It is in our darkest moments that we discover just how powerful our light burns and we realize our potential, regardless of what we face, is limitless. As you read the following account of where I am now, I respectfully ask that you remember I stand before you vulnerable, proud of the man I am, and humbly appreciative of the second chance I was presented with. I also represent proof of concept. None of us are bound to the labels thrust upon us, nor prisoners to the grim fate of said labels.

For years I was asked to write an epilogue. However, even I, experiencing my recovery, doubted that I was truly through the worst of it, and doubted that I was truly done with it, or rather that it was done with me. How could I possibly have stumbled onto something that the world wasn't aware of? Why was I granted a second chance when so many of those I knew with the same struggles were faltering? These were important questions that I needed time to analyze and assess before returning to tell the world that I was indeed, without a doubt, beyond the bipolar that had threatened everything I had ever desired. I was certainly not the only one who doubted my story.

Even after four years of proven stability with Dr. Simon, all documented, when he took the retirement he so deserved, I was suddenly without an advocate. Searching for a doctor who was willing to research my case and prescribe off-label medication was my first authentic test of stability. Medical professionals have a duty to protect their patients, and although I understood their fear when seeing bipolar on my medical chart, I didn't understand why they couldn't see what was typed in bold at the top of my medical chart: "FULL REMISSION FROM BIPOLAR I." It was a startling reminder of the stigma caused by mental health, and it was both frustrating and demoralizing at times.

I went to doctors who refused to prescribe the medications that had changed my life for the better. I faced off against those who looked at me— someone without a fancy degree—as a failure, charlatan, and perhaps even a danger to the paradigm they'd ascribed to their entire medical careers. I even had one doctor, a graduate of Harvard, who refused to call my previous doctor for verification and records. The woman I was with at the time was a nurse. After listening to the way this doctor spoke to me, she wanted to file a complaint. I refused to. What good would come of reporting a doctor? I already knew what would be heard. Through the sound of stigma and discrimination, the complaint would only be seen as "a manic episode," and I wasn't going to let anyone pull me down any longer.

The truth was that every wall I faced was nothing compared to bipolar. Every doubter fueled my desire to prove myself, not for my own ego, but for the countless others I knew were suffering in silence. I could shoulder the burden of proof required of me. Without any medical tests to prove that I had overcome bipolar, I knew the only way to truly break into the world of science was with compassion, calm, and indisputable proof of stability. In many ways, I thank the cruelest of the medical professionals I faced for helping me strive to be the best version of myself.

Realizing that the path to proving myself was a far taller mountain than I had ever dreamed of climbing, I began a new journey of living my life to prove *exactly* what a stable mind can accomplish. If I needed to be perfect to lead doctors and researchers in new avenues, I would strive for perfection. If the voiceless had no one to stand atop a hill and inspire, I would shout until my voice or life faded. In short, I had already made a choice to stand out when I originally published the memoir: I would dedicate my life to helping others, instilling hope, working with medical professionals, and providing an ear and voice to those that had yet to break free of the struggles, stigmas, and pains they couldn't verbalize.

Armed with the knowledge that escaping the chains of bipolar was the easy part of my end goal, I began on Twitter. "@Chaos2Cured" remains my social media handle, and I utilize every platform as proof of stability and as a living journal that can easily be referenced. I did not begin posting out of a desire to join the social media community, but because I knew that no one would believe the claims unless they could *see* the results. If a picture was worth a thousand words, I needed my life to stand for more. My life *had* to succeed. Not only for me, but for each and every person that didn't get the second chance I did.

As I began posting, I was asked to be a guest on a podcast. It was my first recorded interview and it was with the wonderful Lisa Davis, now someone I call a friend and advocate of all humans. Quickly, one interview led to others, none of them paid, but the currency I was looking for wasn't money… I needed a platform. If posting was one form of proof of consistency, why not allow others to hear my voice and see me in action. Visibility was key and something I continue to improve at.

Shortly after my first interview, I was interviewed by Tiffany Werhner, host of "Moments of Clarity with Tiffany." She was an award nominated, board-certified psychologist who hosted a live radio show in Tampa, Florida. Skeptical and cautious, especially on a live platform where an out-of-control guest could get her and the station fined by the FTC, she gave me a chance. The interview was a success, and eventually led to a love of public speaking. The more I spoke of my struggles, the more people reached out to share and thank me for my openness.

I was hardly a celebrity, nor did I want such status, but I did want my message spread loud and far. Hope was something the world needed, especially those in the mental health realm. I also needed it, for my journey was one I had no one to speak with or understand. As the first person to be medically documented with remission due to my protocol, I often felt alone and terrified as emotions I had never felt bubbled to the surface. Although many wanted to know how I was doing and even asked for a second book, I first had to face a world without bipolar. Yes, that sounds easy, but when 'normal' emotions and experiences left me startled or even breathless, I promised myself I wouldn't write an epilogue or second book until I was fully ready. I needed one hundred percent certainty that I could write each and every word with the power of truth and knowledge that I had, in fact, risen above my past struggles, as well as the new ones I faced.

To this day, I am still learning how to deal with emotions that I didn't grow up with. Unique struggles continued to surprise me as bipolar became a distant memory. My anxiety, ADHD, and OCD became far more prevalent as bipolar was no longer able to mute them with mania or depression. Fear, love, and even sympathy were new emotions that had steep learning curves that often felt overwhelming.

For example, I still remember the first time I truly cried. Let me be crystal clear: I had shed tears before, but they were always shallow or manipulative. Although I had felt overwhelming sadness with depression, I had never truly felt a real reason to cry. Pain was simply part of my life due to the linear IgA that continues to light my skin on fire, and I had lost loved ones, but I will never forget the first time I cried with my heart. To say it was unexpected and overwhelming is an understatement. It was in the movie **Up** by Pixar, and the sadness I felt at the beginning of the movie still shakes me enough I have not rewatched it. When I felt such deep emotions, it was both terrifying and beautiful all at once. It was the first time I realized that, although bipolar had torn my life apart, it had also offered protections. This is extremely important for one truth: no matter what you face, there are positives that you can find. Even in the deepest of despair or pain, there is something good you can learn or grasp onto in order to keep hope alive.

Other emotions like fear or uncertainty were something I hadn't had to face like most do. For example, when I began painting, it was with furious abandon. Strokes of the paintbrush would sweep across the canvas as if alive. I did not see colors the way I do now, so many of them were overly bright. Now, long after I took my life back, I feel hesitation and a small amount of fear with every stroke. Living or acting without fear had been a great positive bipolar had provided, and things like doubt had never presented itself. Now, each and every day I face fear, anxiety, doubt, and hesitation like anyone else. However, instead of seeing that as a negative, I view it as a beauty of the human experience.

Painting was not the only activity that saw a startling change. Everything from dating, cooking, and indeed every aspect of my life saw a dramatic metamorphosis as I grew more stable with each passing day, week, month, and year. One thing that continues to help me, and I advocate for all, is neuroplasticity. It is a proven concept that we can, with great and continual effort, rewire our own mind. This is something I needed in order to overcome the many trials I faced after coming out of the coma bipolar had left me with. I use the aforementioned sentence with clear intent. Some people view my recovery with rose colored glasses, but make no mistake, I awoke to a world that didn't accept me. I had no university degree to use to pole vault into a high-earning career, I felt old, and at the same time I felt immature and in need of life experience. I also found relationships of all kinds both beautiful and, at times, bewildering.

While I used to see every person as an enemy trying to cause pain, use me, or manipulate me, it was startling to see that humans were kind and loving. Are they all the time? Certainly not, but I absolutely believe that every person is born with the capacity for love and kindness at their core. This belief and realization was very confusing for me to face. I was in my mid-thirties and I hadn't ever truly trusted someone. The new me made mistakes, trusted the wrong people, and I suffered my first experiences with heartache and pain. Each moment of learning through this pain and confusion was challenging, but compared to feeling nothing for my fellow human, the pain was a welcome reminder of how cold and calculating I once was, and just how far I'd come. I was slowly learning to appreciate the human weaknesses that I had once looked down upon with disgust. Without pain, how can we understand, or fathom, bliss?

As I faced a new life with what felt like a brand new mind, I felt insecurities that I never had before, but also childlike excitement at the most mundane. A blender with a button that lit up was something I wanted to share with my loved ones. Rewatching movies and shows felt like watching them for the first time, and simple joys like food amazed my senses. I could have chosen to be overwhelmed by life, by the setbacks that weren't completely my fault, but I didn't have a choice. To prove my worth, to prove to the world that I had indeed overcome the unthinkable, I had only one choice: embrace everything I faced with enthusiasm while granting myself grace when I stumbled. Failing forward, a military term, became something of a mantra for me. If I had no one to talk with, I would face my fear as if I still had bipolar. I would, with all my might, find the good in every moment, every experience, and every failure, learning to shape my thoughts, and in the process, shaping my mental fitness.

In a long relationship where I had to help care for another was another test of my stability. To live with another, to be a foundation that lifted another as I held a job, spread my message, and faced the uncertainty of life was both challenging and entertaining. I began to realize that if I couldn't conquer a situation, I could use it to strengthen me. Much like a muscle or bone, stress and even minor damage led to growth and more strength. The most fascinating part of my embracing challenges was how life connected me with amazing people.

It wasn't just people that felt my change. My dogs instantly felt the change in the energy I carried with each step. I had always understood animals more than people, mostly because they never hide their intent. The openness and honesty of communication between animals was something I aspired to duplicate in the human experience. Although it failed often, the more honest I was with myself and those I loved and cared for, the more inner-peace I felt. For example, as I write this epilogue, I feel a sense of justice, honor, compassion, and truth being written with each stroke of my keyboard. With every breath I live as I want to be remembered. I could care less about the "things" in life. The only thing that truly matters to me is the legacy I leave in the wake of my existence.

As the years passed by, I began to understand that the things I thought always mattered in life were simply not that important. A fancy car means nothing if your life isn't something you're proud of, just as the number of zeros in a bank account can't erase a legacy of damage and pain. Put in the most simplistic of ways, the better I felt, the more stable I was, and the further I stepped from the bipolar that once defined me, the more I desired to leave footprints others who were suffering could use as stepping stones to a better and more beautiful life.

One of the questions I am often asked, especially when I speak, is how I face each day. How do I take on life, especially when it comes to work, stability, physical health, medication, and facing doubt? Not only is it a question I love, but I also feel the question is something that must be answered carefully with complete truth and enthusiasm.

First of all, to believe that anything is easy for anyone is a logical fallacy. We all face difficulties we must overcome. That is not only part of life, but my struggles have become a key component to driving me to a more successful and positive person. When I choose to focus on the positive aspects of a difficulty I am faced with the solution, strategy, or end result. Facing the challenge becomes more of a game and less of a drive of panic, frustration, or even despair.

When I first began facing my anxiety, OCD, and normality after bipolar was behind me, I was extremely negative. Schedule changes were emotionally draining, compulsions would often make me feel powerless, and panic attacks would leave me gasping for air. No longer oblivious to my financial responsibilities and aware that I was behind where I wanted to be, I couldn't allow panic, fear, or helplessness keep me from steady work. I wanted to succeed, but I had not ever really had an opportunity. One thing I knew for certain was that I would not waste the second chance I had been given. So, I looked for solid and proven solutions, ranging from cognitive behavioral therapy to meditation. My search led me to something called neuroplasticity.

As someone who had always enjoyed bodybuilding, the idea that I could help shape, tone, and rewire my mind was not only fascinating, but something I wanted to delve into. It was a slow process, but worth every second. The idea was more simplistic than the execution. Instead of allowing my brain to process something in a negative or stressful way, I would catch the thought and focus on finding even a shred of positivity to reframe my perspective.

Instead of feeling like my time was short, I would focus on how much time I did have. Instead of getting angry at a mistake, I would focus on what I could learn from the experience. It was extremely difficult to do, and I still have a long way to go to reach my goals, however, each attempt made the next easier. The more I continued to shape my mental fitness, the easier it was to simply face the real world.

After years of being unable to hold a job or even function, I suddenly found myself calm, positive, and working with a few students. What began as a few grew with every passing year. My existing talents became easier to explain and enhance, and, although I never again want to do it again, I worked for over fourteen hundred days straight. If someone wanted to see stability, I now have hundreds of students and families that rely on me for the formative years and I won't let them down.

Toning my mind and building a foundation of acceptance for my flaws was just one factor in what helped me continue to improve and build a happier life. Other key factors that allowed my mental training to peak were things like diet, water intake, and sleep. Study after study showed the importance of setting a consistent sleeping schedule, something I admit was not my strongest desire, yet imperative for mental health and strength. Fish oil, natural anti-inflammatories, and healthy diet further aided my body's ability to change and evolve into a vessel more adept at remaining calm. (**To anyone wondering how to get started on this, most certified therapists can give tools to get you started. It is also important to remember to take things one step at a time and never compare your progress to another's. We all change and grow at different rates, so there is no benefit of comparison.**)

With each passing year, I grew more confident and happier with the person I was becoming. There were always trials, but those trials gave me an opportunity to prove just how efficient I had become. My work flowed and suddenly I had students winning at the state level with violin, while at the same time my bank account was finally growing. Eventually, I had one struggle that remained: my self-vision.

I saw myself as a lesser person for a very long time. After being told so many times that there was no hope and that bipolar would rule my life, even when the health professionals were trying to inspire hope, what I heard was that I would never be me. I would never have an identity outside of the label I had already risen above and defeated. It was about two years after I published my memoir when I began a friendship with a wonderful woman named Dr. Denise McDermott.

As a psychiatrist, Dr. Denise had to work within the scope of the medical license she had. After years of practice, helping thousands, she coined the term NeuroStyle. The idea was both simplistic and beautiful to me. When we first spoke, she never referred to my bipolar. Instead, she focused on the person I was, the way I perceived the world, and the grace with which I had stepped above the struggles that had once nearly drowned me in shadows.

I could write an entire book on this, and we will, but I will leave this brief for the purpose of remaining on point. When we let go of the labels and see ourselves as humans with endless potential and ability to shape who we wish to be, we may never reach every dream we desire to achieve, but we can enjoy the journey, and, most importantly, recapture the potential we all have within.

No matter what I faced, I found that as long as I kept pushing towards becoming stronger, more stable, and leaving a legacy I would be proud of, the warmer I felt and the more powerful my next day potential became. We can't shape each and every outcome, but we can certainly shape how we view the things that happen to us. When we can see a broken leg as an opportunity to strengthen the bone, enhance the muscles around it, and improve how our body responds, why would we assume we can't do the same for our mind? Truth is we can, which is why I will never use the words mental illness. If anything, the very worst situations are a mental *difference,* and until we rid the world of shame and stigma for suffering and struggles no one can control, humanity will continue to misunderstand the human condition and mind. Instead, I want us to all see the human mind as it always has been: an endless potential that can be used to inspire and build a better world and future for the individual and the community.

Even as I write this, I feel lighter and more inspired to continue onwards. I bring this up last because I almost forgot to mention that the right intentions, pure and honorable, have helped me move forward. Although I often fail to be exactly who I want to be and frustration sometimes overtakes me, remaining focused on being an example for myself, my loved ones, and forging a pathway of light, love, and hope, allows me to stay steadfast in my goals and progress.

After years of being asked exactly how I am doing, I thought it was important to reiterate that we all move at our own pace. Achievement, to me, isn't about stature or money, but about my ability to lay down at the end of the day and be proud of all I did that day. Some days, that might only be getting up and cleaning. The success isn't measured by the grandness of the accomplishment, but that another day was faced, battled, and survived.

Let's face it, just surviving life is a challenge, but challenges are fun. That's why we play games, why we compete, why we strive to become better. When we realize the point of life isn't about winning some prize of wealth and fame, but about finding success in the smallest of actions, it becomes possible to enjoy so much more or the little things we forget to appreciate.

All that I have written above is not only who I am on a daily basis, but who I want to remain and be remembered for. Reframing my life, toning and rebuilding my mind, all allowed me to find continual stability and success. It is also why in 2021, after facing a pandemic that tested each and every pillar of my stability, I was nominated for multiple mental health advocacy awards; my fantasy book, thick with mental health symbolism, was nominated for best new fantasy; and every student that competed placed in the top three at the state level. The icing on the cake was placing second in my division for Mr. Health and Fitness, 2021.

I once had doubts about who I was and if I could ever reach the person I wanted to be. Those doubts still linger but fade further from my thought process with every breath I take. As for my treatment protocol, there are over fifty pharmaceutical patents claiming the medications I use could be useful in mood-stabilization, and a meta study, published in 2019 (need to insert article name and credits here) only strengthened my claims about tamoxifen citrate and bipolar.

I know that I am a long way from accomplishing what I set out to do, but a journey is different than a destination. I don't care when I reach my goal, whether in this lifetime or the next, because I know that fighting towards it is more important to the legacy I choose to leave behind me. Of course, I strive to finish all I set out to accomplish, but I have spent the majority of my life unable to appreciate anything in life, even colors. To do anything less than embrace the second chance I have and do all I can to love each and every moment would only cheapen something grand.

In summary, and the only take-away I wish for someone reading this book to carry with them is this: no matter what your life was, no matter what label you were given, *you* have the ability to take control. I do not mean to imply this is easy, but why would anyone want the easy path? It is our scars, wrinkles, and imperfections that make us sparkle with beauty and potential. Our natural talents and skills are simply easier to embrace. It is when we embrace our imperfections and weaknesses, insistent about conquering them, that the light we need warms and brightens our path forward.

You are never alone in your journey and there is *no* room for shame in our struggles. Learn to embrace the beauty that is you and own your label. I don't see myself as bipolar any longer. I only see who I am and what I will continue to fight for. Where once I was held back, my wings are now free of the chains that bound them and I will fly high, not for my own glory, but so that I can spread hope further. What I once was is lost to the past, and I will forever be grateful for even the worst moments in my life. I would beg the same of anyone facing a mental health diagnosis.

Do not fear what you are. Embrace it, use it, and build a legacy that even time, and the heavens can't tear down.

Mr. Kirk Patrick Miller is available for keynote speaking, radio, or consultation.

www.ingramcontent.com/pod-product-compliance
Lightning Source LLC
Chambersburg PA
CBHW060932140726
47996CB00001B/470